CULTURALLY RELEVANT TEACHING

AND

LEARNING FOR SUCCESS

[FIRST EDITION]

By C.T. Wilson

cognella®
academic publishing

Bassim Hamadeh, CEO and Publisher
Michael Simpson, Vice President of Acquisitions
Jamie Giganti, Senior Managing Editor
Miguel Macias, Graphic Designer
Zina Craft, Senior Field Acquisitions Editor
Gem Rabanera, Project Editor
Elizabeth Rowe, Licensing Coordinator
Allie Kiekhofer, Interior Designer

ISBN: 978-1-63487-132-7 (pbk) / 978-1-63487-133-4 (br)

www.cognella.com   800-200-3908

[CONTENTS]

INTRODUCTION

"It was the eyes ... ." I blinked and tilted my head to the side, revealing the universal, nonverbal message to tell me more.

"See, his eyes told me a story an eight-year-old should not have known existed, let alone tell. He had an emotionless face that revealed little, but those eyes ... those eyes showed me everything," my friend whispered to me in restrained horror as he described not a scene from a dreadful accident where the surviving child just learned his parents were violently snatched from the living, but rather one who was called upon to read a passage from the text in class. Yet, the palpable terror of the little brown boy my friend shared, although secondhand, seemed all the same.

Alexander, as I will call my friend, explained he was traveling with a well-known local politician who was visiting a rural, poor, Southern school in his district to highlight the importance of reading in this new STEM economy.

"Reading," the politician said, "was integral to a child's success in school and life, and we should do all we can to make sure that they are prepared to be model citizens in our society." Alexander said to himself, "How about we start by making sure they are not terrified to be in school." Society's model, after all, begins in school.

But who was Alexander kidding, while the school was mixed demographically, the white children were not terrified to read aloud, or even attempt to, poorly. On the contrary, in a place that is supposed to be safe for learning, creating, and exploring, something traumatic gripped the young brown boy when the school's teacher of the year called on him.

To read.

Something that he had been doing since kindergarten.

While there are a number of possible variables that could have contributed to the young man's temporary paralysis, there seemed to be more evidence of an environment that spoke to both Alexander's and my suspicions. The young brown boy, without Alexander or the oblivious politician having visited the classroom, for more than two minutes had illuminated a serious and discernible observation: the brown boy *was not* welcome.

To his classmates he was different, yet he looked just like the rest: an eight-year-old.
He was an alien in a place where he should be welcome, celebrated for his own potential. Yet he sat there, petrified.

Was this a function of him or the environment created for ... no, *against* him?

I asked Alexander more. He explained the young brown boy sat in the back of the classroom, isolated and visibly alone. Yet his desk was equidistant from the others. Other brown children dotted the classroom, but curiously nothing on the bulletin boards acknowledged their historical or contemporary existence. It was, Alexander uncomfortably joked, as if the brown kids were visiting a foreign country's children's art museum. Alexander and I talked more and he remembered that in doing the prep work for the visit, the data of the school revealed that while forty percent of the students were minorities, eighty percent of their teachers were white.

The teacher called out the brown boy's full name as if reminding him that he had a name was going to kick-start him.

It just embarrassed him more, Alexander lamented.

After the excruciating fifteen seconds had passed, the teacher of the year moved on to the next student who stammered through the text, but finished and popped his head up for approval, exclaiming "George Washington was the best American ever!"

The classroom erupted in agreement.
The young brown boy's head sank.
The principal quickly whisked Alexander and the politician to the next classroom.

That was 2010.

People say that the world is a small place.
The South is smaller.

A few years later, I am talking to a teacher friend about the Moral Monday protests in North Carolina. With CNN blaring in the background at our favorite cafe, Judy turned and confided in me by saying, "The legislators are going to pay off the teachers. Just watch. And the kids are going to suffer. They don't care about them and sadly they know it." Unable to adequately challenge her words, an awkward and painful silence settled over our coffee as a nondescript news anchor spilled out talking points that subtly did more to discreetly question the movement rather than cover it.

In an annoyance by Judy's unrelenting cynicism that I couldn't contain, I blurted out "Prove it!"

She coyly invited me to school on the following Monday. I accepted.

I arrived at a familiar rural Southern elementary school early that Monday and settled in to observe Judy's routine. She is an Exceptional Children's teacher and explains that she is often hurt as she sees normal young brown boys get labeled with behavioral disabilities. She argues their true ability is often masked by the negativity from the teachers who simply do not perceive these children as having any value. Oftentimes the students are not disabled at all, just discarded. Judy's students had not arrived in her room for resource time. We overhear a conversation from two obviously frustrated teachers.

One teacher stated that she didn't "know what to do with him; he's lazy and so hostile."

Another teacher interjected "he gives me lip some times, but I tell him it's his choice to succeed, not mine."

Dismissive at best, I thought. With that attitude there was no way the child was going to receive a balanced education that would empower and uplift his whole person.

The conversation quickly hushed as a tall young African American boy bumbled into our classroom. "Hi, Mrs. Williams," he offered politely to Judy. "Hi, mister," as he acknowledged me. Judy responded in kind and I nodded and smiled. Judy darted her eyes to me and said sternly, "Watch." The young man opened the door to the adjoining room and entered the presence of the two unrevealed teachers. I thought, "This young man seems completely normal—I guess you never know."

Several minutes pass and almost like clockwork Judy gets up from her seat and motions to me to join her at the door. There is a slender window and I peer through it with Judy to observe the one-on-one teaching session. Apparently the other teacher left. The young man asked to use the restroom, but his teacher asked him to get out a sheet of paper and a pencil first. He reached in his desk and took out a pencil. He asked again if he could go to the restroom. She replied, "No, you didn't get out any paper." He begged, "I really need to go to the restroom." The teacher then yelled, "NO!" Frustrated, he got up and walked out. We quickly sat back down in our seats to avoid being seen. Then Judy asked me to follow her to the main office to observe what was about to transpire. When we were barely past the threshold of the door, we saw the young man had only made it into the hallway before a white male teacher spotted him and asked him what was he doing out of the class. The teacher rushed into the boy's personal space and yelled that he was acting like a two-year-old. Judy and I turned our backs and pretended that we were discussing a bulletin board that praised the virtues of Thomas Jefferson. The male teacher pointed his finger at the young man and yelled that he needed to show respect. The young man, now visibly squirming, said, "I really need to go to the restroom." The male teacher got in his face and said, "You aren't going to the restroom. You either go back to class or go to the office." Humiliated, the young boy began to cry and asked the man to stop yelling at him. The male teacher said, "Then you show respect." Then, inexplicably, the teacher grabbed the young boy by his t-shirt and began dragging him to the office. Ironically the student is bigger than the teacher. Instead of complying, the young man quickly snatched away and went into his class. By this point, a crowd of teachers and students had gathered, so there was little need for us to mask our intentions. Feeding on the attention, the male teacher proudly said, "I thought so." In an effort to completely emasculate the young man, the male teacher demanded, "Now, you are going to look her (female teacher) in the eyes and tell her you are sorry." The young man kept his head down and said, "I really just need to go to the bathroom." The principal burst in and said, "We are not dealing with this, we are going to call the police." His main teacher rushed in and immediately asked the young man what was going on and what did he need to do. He said, "I need to go to the restroom and I had to get out paper and a pencil but I don't have any paper." The main teacher furiously exclaimed "You don't have any paper … really?"

Even now, instead of allowing the young man to go to the restroom, the male teacher told him he had to ask his teacher for some paper, the caveat being that he must "look her in her eyes and say, please." Instead of being humiliated once more, the student got up, visited the restroom, and walked to the office. The police were immediately called and his mother informed that he was being defiant.

As a consummate and perpetual researcher of our public schools, I walked down to the office to observe the interaction of the mother, the young man, and police from afar. They were not given an office to adjudicate this process in private; instead they were relegated to the hallway.

The boy's first name was very common, his last is not.

The police officer used it often to refer to his mother after "Miss" although she wore a wedding ring set.

"That name …" I pondered.
I froze.
The boy happened to be that same brown boy from 2010.

This is 2013.

How did we get here?

Where will we go?

Where will he go?

I remember when I looked my child in the eyes for the first time. I knew then I would give absolutely anything to ensure her success and security.

It was love, it is humanity.

I know in this economy, for the future, that success and security, long after I am gone, is going to depend on her ability to earn a living for herself. That is going to require education. A good balanced education that speaks to her soul and her experience.

While there is no question parental love is required from each teacher for every student who walks through a school door, we parents entrust our state and private entities to exhibit a level of humanity to each child.

This is simply not occurring from classroom to classroom. Certainly not from child to child. We have problems in this country. We know this.

There is a dominant culture that too often, purposefully or not, over-shadows others. That culture of dominance is dangerous. It creates and fosters confusion, mistrust, mismanagement, disproportionate discipline, expectancy bias, and many other elements that turn a school into a foreign entity to too many. We know what culturally relevant teaching is. We know its power, its purpose, and its theory.

Dr. Gloria Ladson-Billings has created a method of teaching and prac-tice that posits students can be taught brilliantly to achieve without losing their cultural integrity, coining it "Culturally Relevant," which emphasizes respect, value, and empowerment as key elements. But the purpose of this introduction is not to provide you an introductory essay on why it is important.

This piece is an effort to appeal to your humanity, to provide understand-ing of what happens when we collectively ignore the beauty of diversity and culture in our country.

We force a multidimensional world into one lens.

We lose sight.

We lose understanding.

We lose humanity.

We whisper to our precious children every night, "Good night, baby, go to sleep so you can have a good day at school."

But how often do our children shudder with fear and frustration when we mention that word, "school"?

Because school, to them, is a place where they spend seven of twelve to fourteen of their waking hours, is not a place FOR them. Together as a society have to change that narrative.

This book will show you how.

A child cannot be taught by anyone who despises him,
and a child cannot afford to be fooled.

—James Baldwin

AUTHOR'S NOTE

If you are reading this, chances are you bought the book. Thank you. I have been wanting to write a timely piece about diversity, teaching, and learning for several years. I am grateful for this outlet. As an educator, I practice truth. I tell it. I receive it. I honor it. In truth, I probably was not a great teacher. I loved doing it, the interaction with the students is so raw and often gritty, it made me think; instead of me making them better, on several occasions, they made me better. In meeting my students every single year, I had goals, lofty dreams of success and hoping their knowledge base would expand.

Excited before each new school year began, even if I looped with my students, I wanted to know what they did over the summer, how they had grown, and if they retained any of the information imparted to them mere weeks before. Some shocked me, some surprised me, some did not return. Entering the practice and profession of teaching, I realized a great deal about myself and the system of education. I was elitist and the system was greatly flawed. My students beautifully taught me that not everyone wants to go to college or have a big house or get married. Some, they told me, wanted to "keep it simple" and be a carpenter, plumber, or mechanic. More than anything, they wanted acceptance and someone to appreciate their ideals. It wasn't until I began to read about, study, and investigate other practices of teaching that I knew how to make my learning environment diverse and meet their needs. In my seeking, I found Dr. Ladson-Billing's *Culturally Relevant Teaching*. The premise changed my life. It changed my teaching, too.

All students, young and old, come to learn. As a result of their experiences, often these students are already suspicious or untrusting of school. Teachers in the past demeaned them, belittled them, or sat them in corners for hours—and forgot them. Those students have been in and out of Special Education, sometimes foster care, some have hard lives, some are rich, but all have been turned away; turned out by our education system and practices.

As I worked in different school districts, I noticed a curious case of injustice … it looked different everywhere, but not. More African American boys were suspended. More African Americans were in Special Education. More African Americans had difficulty coming to school daily. I was shocked—but not. I loved school. It was a great pleasure to attend daily. I wanted to see friends, read new stories; daily, I waited with great anticipation to hate math and the teacher … I just wanted to be in school. To my shock and surprise, it was difficult for me to comprehend that most students do not feel that way. In several of those homes, survival was the focus, not education. I had to learn not to judge, but teach with understanding. That is the purpose of this book—to teach and unfold practices with understanding. It matters not if this is being used in a remedial course, a course for diversity, a course for preparing future educators, or a simple read; the purpose is to learn to understand the difference and bridge the gap without hatred, without demeaning and belittling.

With that in mind, Chapter One introduces and reminds readers of the origin of K–12 in America. It was not designed for anyone but white boys. Families taught children how to read and write using an alphabet with examples from the Bible. When formalized schooling began, it was male centered. When women were allowed, they were taught etiquette and household practices. African Americans, Asian Americans, Mexican/Latino/Cuban/Hispanic Americans or Native Americans were not thought to be invited or purposeful in the education or training. This practice of leaving children behind or not including people began the practice of racism in schools. Chapter One outlines how the education system began and was implemented, and what its purpose was. Additionally, Chapter One continues and examines the purpose and practices of higher education in America—who created it and how. Again, male dominance prevails.

As the years unfold, the creation of Historically Black Colleges and Universities (HBCUs) and other minority-serving institutions open as the need for educating minorities grows. In this growth and development, the fight for equality and funding demonstrates the racial disparity. Readers will see the clash and the resistance to allow minorities to have educational facilities. The innovation of colleges and universities to serve African Americans is rarely taught. This concept revealed to a struggling reader, diversity thought leader or student, or a new teacher may be the constant reminder and companion of understanding how the inequalities have always been ever-present, yet people have overcome it using their creative minds, coming together, and representing a cause. Their efforts have yielded great results, as HBCUs are a vital part of the higher education community.

Chapter Two begins to tell a story—my story—of what I heard and saw as a teacher and an administrator. It also details the reform movement. As a teacher, I needed Culturally Relevant Teaching practices to relate to my students and to ensure they had some glimpses of success. As my position changed, I also saw that other teachers needed to understand the tenets of CRT and Culturally Mediated Instruction.

Oppressed people often do not know they are oppressed. Mired in the dire need to survive, often parents do not have time to create and build relationships with their child's teacher. Yes, there are some who are "super moms" and find a way to do everything right, all the time, but others are often intimidated by school, its language, the perception of principals and teachers. This appears to the school community parents do not care. Quite the opposite is true. This chapter examines the barriers parents face and how those barriers impact the child. Using Culturally Relevant Teaching often erases the barriers for parents and students. Chapter Two delves deeply into the theory and practice of Culturally Relevant Teaching and unpacks the need and how to implement it in the classroom.

Chapter Four introduces the tenets with concepts of how to implement Culturally Relevant Teaching in the learning environment. Teachers are critical and key in its implementation. Entering the classroom, teachers must leave bias and preconceived notions to teach effectively. Once ostracized, students often remain there, refusing to allow that teacher to teach them. Teachers, entering the learning environment, should also take into consideration that racism, privilege, and extreme barriers remain. This chapter offers an assessment for teachers to gauge their biases honestly and alone. Once those are revealed, this chapter demonstrates how to teach in a way that all students feel positive about learning and engagement.

Finally, Chapter Four holds students and parents accountable. It outlines how to prepare for the learning environment on every level. It is not enough to blame the teacher or for the teacher to blame the student. Learning is critical. Especially in elementary years and remediation. This chapter shows students how to approach the learning setting and how to get their needs addressed.

Overall, this book hopes to inspire different educational practices. Let's have the conversation about education disparity and why certain schools have money and others have none. Let's have the conversation about why African Americans and Hispanics all too often are shuttled and housed in Special Education programs instead of teachers finding ways to incorporate their learning styles. Let's begin to actually implement and demonstrate high-level teaching that yields critical thinkers without regard to zip code, mother's education, father's presence, and tracking. (It's not called tracking anymore.)

As you read, please understand this is written through my lens, my experience. There are several experiences that are different or like my own.

CHAPTER ONE

THE NEED FOR REFORM

Introduction

It is often difficult in the twenty-first century for people to believe America has a racist past. As this is written, we have the first African American President of the United States, women are leaders in major corporations, hold offices, have been Secretary of State, and hold various key leadership positions—outside of education and the home. We see the perceived emergence of African Americans and one Supreme Court Justice is a woman of Hispanic/Latino descent. Once the covers are pulled back and the truth exposed, we see a different America—an America that once did not allow women to attend school; an America that did not allow any minorities to attend school.

Thinking on that, then imagine that America, once forced, said you can attend schools, but the books and facilities will not be like another group's. Understand in that space, more African Americans were educated than not. In the time of strife, people pulled together to really garner better possibilities—some even died so others (you and I) could attend schools in equality. Attend schools of choice—and play sports with everyone, sit in class with everyone, and compete—equally with everyone.

Now think about what you have done with that opportunity. Have you made it your best? Or when you entered the classroom, did you find yourself in front of too many people who did not understand you, try to understand you, or care about your success? Perhaps you encountered excellent teachers with great intentions—and forced you toward your most awesome goals? Either way, education is the key to empowerment, to learning and growing—and it is mandatory. This chapter will provide a brief, yet thorough, overview of the history of K–12 education and higher education. Understand that history can be dark; once learned, it must be held in the minds and hearts of people so it will not be repeated.

Overview of American Secondary Education

In the early decades of America, a large majority of the citizens were not overly concerned with formal education since most work largely incorporated agriculture. The adults taught their children important life lessons and good quality work habits necessary for life on plantations and farms (Good, 1999). Education in America during the colonial years was very simple efforts to teach reading, writing, and basic math.

Although school did have a place in America, large inequalities existed in the system. Schools were attended by children of the wealthy who could stay in school for longer periods of time due to their parents' ability to finance their education. Additionally, these children were not needed to assist their parents or families in the upkeep of the farm or any work-related duties. The poor children, on the other hand, could not consider attending school, as they were needed for labor.

Questions

1. Think about K–12 education today. How has poverty impacted teaching and learning?
2. What gaps still exist today?
3. Think about the role of the colonial parent. Think about the role of the parent in the 1980s and the role parents play today. How are these roles alike; different? What is the most compelling difference?

It was argued in the 1800s that common schooling would serve to ensure that all Americans obtain, free of charge, a formal education. Education reformers were hopeful that this would teach citizens to be responsible, prepare them for a trade or profession, and work to "break down class barriers while providing an opportunity for intellectual growth and from biased doctrines" (Allen-Mears, Washington & Welch, 2000, p. 2). John Dewey (1916) established a concept for education. Thinking that education was a necessity for everyone, he established a set of guidelines of responsibilities for schools. Dewey argued schools should give direction and be a center for growth, where the environment guides the student. Using the environment, education should teach and prepare students for social function, democracy, and thinking.

Questions

1. Are schools preparing students for social function, democracy, and thinking?
2. Are teachers prepared to teach student how to think, how to behave in social functions, and how to participate in democracy?

In spite efforts of common schooling by Dewey and other reformers, most African Americans were still living an enslaved existence, which did not allow any access to formal education. While African Americans and other ethnic minority groups attempted to live with whites in a desegregated manner, in 1896, the US Supreme Court ruled in favor of separate but equal in the *Plessy v. Ferguson* case. This case allowed African Americans to be formally educated, but not with their white counterparts. The US Supreme Court, with this decision, began a practice of undermining fair and equal treatment of minorities in educational settings. As a result of this court ruling, which pervaded the American South for more than fifty years, African Americans and whites were kept away from each other in education, neighborhoods; this was the pathway for Jim Crow Laws. Additionally, what were perceived as the best educational facilities were inaccessible to African Americans and other minorities.

At the turn of the century, high schools were accessible mostly to those individuals who were college bound (Codding, Rothman, & Tucker, 1999). As time progressed, Americans began to regard education as a solution to many social problems. An example of this is the shift from an agriculture-based lifestyle to an industrial and technological society. The Industrial Revolution forced educators to examine the purpose of education and how students should be educated. More Americans started moving to big cities, seeking better opportunities to work at higher wages. These jobs required the ability to handle machinery. In the 1900s, three quarters of the workforce were expected to work in large factories using more of their physical strength, still showing a degree of acuity (Codding, Rothman & Tucker, 1999). What emerged as a result of the new machinery was the need for workers to have literacy skills. These skills did not develop their ability to think logically, critically, or incisively, or to obtain jobs in factories and plants. High schools were needed to teach the minimum requirements to ensure employment.

Questions

1. Think about your high school experience. Did it prepare you for work or college?
2. Did high school teach you how to think critically, logically, or incisively? If so, what were the methods or strategies?

The quality of education remained unequal and it was evident a class structure existed in spite of the country's need for an educated society. Families with better financial resources continued to have better access to a higher quality education. As a result, their children were placed in a position to extend their education for improved mobility without placing their families in economic peril. High schools, at that time, had three tracks: one for the elite who would later take leadership positions in society, one for those training in the skills trades, and one for everyone else. Individuals with the least opportunity to obtain a quality education were those who took on frontline jobs offered in factories (Codding, Rothman & Tucker, 1999).

Questions

1. While tracking was eliminated from several school systems as a practice to streamline students, what is the new tracking strategy used in K–12 schools now?
2. The tracks then were 1) elite 2) training 3) skills/trade; what are the new terms for the three levels of students? Are these accurate or fair? Why or why not?

As time progressed, America entered the era known as The Great Depression. During this time, it was difficult for almost everyone to get an education. Children were not able to attend schools because their families didn't not have enough money for the basic necessities. Many, during this time were malnourished, and schools were forced to close due to lack of funds. Later, to increase enrollment in higher education, the New Deal was established, but it did not provide the financial support needed to sustain the education system.

In the 1940s, Americans grew more concerned with education, or the lack thereof. By the end of WWII, it was discovered that over five million men had not been allowed to provide military services because they were deemed illiterate or educationally deficient (Mondale & Patton, 2001). The under-funded, poorly organized system of secondary education became the opposite during this time. Education was in a period of transition and the federal government involved itself in providing better opportunities for citizens.

In spite of efforts to have access and ability, a tracking system was created. This system was based on the ideals of academic achievement as a function of inherited ability, and only a few are capable of serious learning; the American high school became the gatekeeper, the symbol of socioeconomic barriers and racist practices.

Questions

1. Do you think using high school as a gatekeeper is a racist practice? Why or why not?
2. What is the current gatekeeper in K–12 education?
3. How do teachers/professors aid in the gatekeeper process?
4. How can teachers/professors stop the process?

Overview of American Higher Education

It is important, I believe, for students without regard to their intended discipline to understand what higher education is and how it was formed. Once that is understood, they can find their place in it. While the history is not inclusive or exciting reading, it allows students to understand the changing landscape and offers some points of conversation. For teachers, this provides insight to history they need to know and understand, and hopefully explains how to approach teaching and learning.

Brief History and Overview of American Higher Education

The United States Higher Education system has been deeply influenced by England. As colonists left England, their systems, cultures, and ideals of education were molded by their exposure to the European traditions. More specifically, Oxford and Cambridge set the design and framework for higher education in America (Rudy, 1976). Instead of creating a new system, replication of an old system was easier and trusted.

Harvard, the first American college, was funded by the general court of Massachusetts (Lucas, 2006). Harvard College was modeled after Emmanuel Church, and was established educate clergy (Brubacher & Rudy, 1976; McDade, 2003). The purpose of Harvard was to culturally prepare men for leadership in America.

Soon after, several colleges—The College of William and Mary, the Collegiate School of New Haven (Yale), the College of Philadelphia (University of PA), the College of New Jersey (Princeton), King's College (Columbia), the College of Rhode Island (Brown), Queens' College (Rutgers), and Dartmouth College (McDade, 2003)—were founded, sharing the same purpose and focus as Harvard. At this time, religion defined colleges. As a result of deep frustration with the religious beliefs of the college, Harvard graduates founded another school, the Collegiate School of New Haven (Lucas, 2006). Several colleges begot other colleges as a result of religious differences. Their resolve was to create or institute new colleges with the same broad ideals, but handled in different manners. While these colleges were formed on religious tenets and re-created schools, the purpose and function of these schools did not waver (Lucas, 2006). Each entity wanted to re-create the best and largest schools of higher learning. During this time, few colleges had admissions requirements.

Unlike secondary education, higher education allowed various members of different socioeconomic backgrounds to enter. While higher education was open, it did not have a great population and had few, if any, women, African Americans, Latinos, or other minorities enrolled (Rudolph, 1962; 1990). Rudolph (1962; 1990) further explains fewer than six hundred students in the seventeenth century attended Harvard College, while Yale's enrollment in 1710 was thirty-six, and fewer than one in a thousand people attended any college prior to 1776. Notably, while the numbers were low, even fewer graduated.

Questions

1. How are colleges different today?
2. What were the admissions requirements for your college?
3. If admission requirements were relaxed now, what impact would that have on your institution? Would you have still attended your current institution or would you have attended another? Why?

The first half of the nineteenth century higher education remained the same. Few changes or additions were made. By the early 1800s, institutions were thought to be well established if they enrolled and retained more than a dozen (12) students. Later, in 1864, Rudolph (1962, 1990) explains most colleges had fewer than 250 students. The cost of tuition was paid by students, while some came on scholarship. As a result of low enrollment and low graduation rates, many institutions found themselves on the brink of bankruptcy (Lucas, 2006). Students were scarce as a result of field labor and women having different roles in society.

Seminaries and schools for women were new additions to the higher education landscape. The first institution for women was Wesleyan Female College in 1836, with Judson College (1836) and Mary Sharp College for Women in 1852 (Rudolph, 1962 & 1990). These colleges suffered early as a result of low enrollment, insufficient endowments, and the thoughts in general about women being educated at that time (McRae, 2003). Again, during this period, few if any, minorities were allowed access to higher education. As a result of slavery, it was a criminal act in the South for African Americans to be formally educated. In 1620, in northern states, many schools were opened by Presbyterians to teach slaves to read and write.

The purpose of higher education from 1850 to 1930, according to Alderson (1998), was to prepare students for public service, vocations, and teaching. Often, due to farming and agriculture, families already trained and prepared their children for a specific vocation and thought education was unnecessary.

The Morrill Acts of 1862 and 1890 made clear that higher education was the responsibility of the public (Alderson, 1988). Because of the overall good of attaining any education enhanced the social and economic dynamics of the person, and was beneficial to the state, it was becoming more acceptable for white males to seek higher education. However, the case of *Plessy v. Ferguson*, according to Lofgren (1987), reduced the 14th Amendment to little more than a pious goodwill resolution and indeed gave the ultimate blow to the Civil War Amendments and the quality of life for black people.

Questions

1. How have race and gender impacted education?
2. What is the 14th Amendment?
3. What are the Civil War Amendments?
4. What was the purpose of the Morrill Act?
5. After reading this, answer the questions below:
6. Was education in the 1800s ever meant to be equal?
7. Were the laws created to aid or hinder the educational development of women and minorities?
8. What were the motives of the leaders at that time?

Between 1880 and 1930, the application of vocational education was emerging. As a result of professional schools and programs, there was an alignment to work and college. The emergence of schools of business, engineering, education, nursing, and social work were defined in higher education. Higher education became responsible for creating and designing programs that would aid in solving social ills of that day.

Post-World War II

The years between 1950 and 1990 showed an expansion of colleges and universities. A major tenet of this increase resulted in the post-World War II expansion. The Serviceman's Readjustment Act of 1944, better known as the GI Bill, and President Truman's Commission on Higher Education Act of 1947 set the terms for growth (McRae, 2003; Alderson 1998). The GI

Bill provided federal aid to veterans to help them easily adjust to civilian life in the areas of medical need, the purchase of homes and businesses, and education. This bill provided for tuition, subsistence, books, supplies, equipment, and counseling services for veterans so they could continue their education, either in high school or college (Gutter, 1986). The number of students—more than 2 million of them veterans—enrolling in colleges and universities skyrocketed; facilities soon became overcrowded, which led to an increasing need for larger classrooms, better equipped laboratories, a greater number of facilities, and more resources.

At this time, students from all socioeconomic backgrounds were being educated in fields such as humanities, agriculture, engineering, commerce, and mining. While college attendance was high, it was not smooth. Critics were doubtful that American higher education was rigorous enough for the Cold War Era (Lazerson, 1998). During the 60s and 70s, there were many demonstrations, protests, and violent reactions that divided higher education institutions (Rudolph, 1962). In the midst of this turbulent time, the Higher Education Act of 1965 created an expanded program of financial aid to include work-study, student grants and loans, and college facility funds to focus on access through need-based grants.

Questions

1. How has financial aid/grants helped with your college tuition?
2. Recently there were changes made in how students can repay their loans—are you familiar with the new rules?
3. How do you think of financial aid? Is it a means to an end or is it allowing too many people into higher education?

An attitude of peril and praise toward the Vietnam War in the late 1960s and early 1970s was witnessed in campus demonstrations. Initial demonstrations were supportive of the war; however, as the war went on, the shift to rebellious anti-war practices became prevalent. In higher education, as a result of the demonstrations and freedom rallies for students, the number of required courses declined and autonomy was given to students in what courses they would take that satisfied the degree (Randolph, 1962). In essence, because of the turmoil, universities transitioned to shorter time in class and college for students to graduate.

The 70s represented a decade that decreased the value of education. Suddenly, tuition rates were high and critics began to openly challenge the quality of teaching and curricula, questioning the depth of learning. This critique allowed legislators to reduce federally funded programs and state spending practices.

Questions

1. How have the higher education landscape and scope changed?
2. How are critics challenging the higher education environment today? What is the difference between the challenges today versus the critics of the 60s, 70s, and 80s?
3. How are you transcending the higher learning environment?

Nontraditional students, who were prominent after World War II and were predominantly returning veterans, re-emerged in the 1980s. "Nontraditional," as a term, was not identified in the student context until this time. Costs to attend college were extremely high, as was college enrollment. This era includes the 1990s, which offered extreme criticism of higher education practices, policies, missions, and outcomes (McDade, 2003; Lazerson, 1988; Rudolph, 1962). As a result of higher minority enrollment, the aging of America, and the redefining of the American family, higher education was changing. Technological advances had also become essential in higher education. If American higher education were to become a competing force internationally, strategic and organizational changes would have to improve.

Questions

1. Is America still competitive internationally?
2. If yes, how long can American higher education remain competitive or relevant if our high schools are underperforming?

The concept of American higher education is unique and different, as its inception was based on a hegemonic system. Based on the concept of democracy, access, and freedom, higher education had to endure several reforms and ideological changes to include everyone while providing an education that personally benefited the student and publicly benefited local, state, and federal initiatives. The expansion of higher education was charged to ensure that all minority groups have equal opportunity and access.

Access to Higher Education

The history of American education is riddled with problems of inclusion and exclusionary practices. Legislative reforms have forced the nation from segregation to integration. These laws created a sub-group of colleges and institutions for minorities. This portion will explore the emergence of minority-serving institutions.

Minority, in this case, is a person or persons who are non-white. The creation of the Morrill Act, which allowed the funding of land grant institutions, was to serve minorities. The flaw in this act is it failed to specify if African Americans would benefit from this funding. This loophole allowed increased access to higher education. The flaw in this established law allowed southern states to create separate higher education institutions, thus identified as minority serving.

Questions

1. What is the Morrill Act?
2. What flaw allowed minorities to attend college or gain access to higher education?
3. Had there been no flaw, how do you think minorities would have been able to access higher education?

Historically Black Colleges and Universities (HBCUs)

The largest body of minority-serving institutions is classified as historically black colleges and universities (HBCUs). There was limited opportunity and access for African Americans in higher education. Before the Morrill Act of 1862, Cheyney University, located in Pennsylvania, was established in 1830, and then Lincoln and Wilberforce in 1850, offering African Americans a chance to earn a college degree. After the Civil War, in 1867, Howard University was federally funded solely for educating African Americans.

The Freedman's Bureau was established to assist African Americans who were seeking a college education (Rudolph, 1962). The bureau attempted to help former slaves, refugees and poor whites improve their opportunities. During this time, several HBCUs opened as a result of the 13th, 14th and 15th Amendments. The 13th Amendment abolished slavery and prohibited slavery and involuntary servitude. Established December 6, 1865 and declared a proclamation by the Secretary of State, William H. Seward signed it into law. Following that, the 14th Amendment was the first post-Civil War Reconstruction Amendment. It was intended to secure the rights of former slaves. Proposed on June 13, 1866 and ratified on July 9, 1868, the 14th Amendment defines citizenship, and overruled the Dred Scott Decision of 1857. The Dred Scott decision had excluded slaves and their descendants from the protection of all Constitutional Rights. This amendment gives equal protection under the law to all persons within their jurisdiction and was used to dismantle racial segregation (McDade, 2003). The 15th Amendment banned race-based voting qualifications and prohibits each government in the United States from preventing a citizen from voting based on race, color, or previous conditions of servitude. This amendment was ratified February 3, 1870. With these amendments, coupled with the work of the Freedman's Bureau, fourteen southern states established 575 schools and employed more than 1,000 teachers (Lazerson, 1988). The need for higher education was evident and an attempt was made to establish enough normal schools to educate teachers.

Questions

1. Why were several schools created for agriculture, education, and farming?
2. What is the Dred Scott Decision and how did it impact the higher education landscape?
3. What was the role of HBCUs when they were created? Do you think that role has changed?
4. What is a normal school?

During the late 1800s, several colleges opened, the most prominent of which was Howard University in 1867. Opened on a federal grant, Howard created eight departments for normal and preparatory coursework, including music, theology, military training, industrial, commercial, college law, and medicine. Creating these departments opened new professional venues for African Americans.

HBCUs continued to grow and flourish throughout the nineteenth century. During this time, more than 200 HBCUs were established and were the only source of higher education for African Americans. Because access was still problematic, several legal cases were fought in regard to equity and access (Lazerson, 1988). Many of the cases were brought to fight to have equal access to higher education without regard to race, sex, or other forms of categorization. The famous cases include *Sweatt v. Painter*, 1950; *MacLaurin v. Oklahoma State Board of Regents*, 1950; *Adams v. Richardson*, 1972; and *United States v. Fordice*, 1992. As a result of losing their fights equality, HBCUs became the largest producers of African American degree holders in the nation (NCES, 2004b). While still facing racial issues in the form of financial equalities, HBCUs still produce quality graduates equal to their white counterparts.

Questions

1. How can HBCUs remain relevant?
2. Should HBCUs change their focus to be more inclusive?
3. Should HBCUs recruit other minority populations?

Hispanic Institutions

HBCUs were created to educate African Americans. Hispanic-serving institutions were first created to serve whites, and as time progressed, began to serve Hispanics as a result of a cultural shift in neighborhoods, schools, and other aspects leading students to higher education. According to the National Center for Education Statistics (NCES) (1997), Hispanic-serving institutions are defined as institutions having an enrollment of undergraduate full-time students that is at least twenty-five percent Latino/Hispanic. Hispanics are the fastest growing population in the United States and it is critical that higher education institutions begin to create programs designed to boost their achievement. Additionally, higher education institutions may need to devise a plan to aid students who are undocumented, but have been educated in the United States.

Questions

1. Why were traditionally white institutions welcoming of Hispanics, but not African American students?
2. Are there any Hispanic-serving institutions now?

Asians and Pacific Islanders in Higher Education

Asians and Pacific Islanders in higher education were recognized in part due to demographics rather than directed missions of institutions to serve that population. Because this section of the population is not readily recognized or funded by the federal government, they are not recognized as needing a "serving institution." However, in 2005, legislation named the Asian American and Pacific Islander Serving Institutions Act was introduced. According to Thor (2005), the purpose of this act was to establish a federal designation for institutions where ten percent or more of the population was Asian or Pacific Islander and low income. This would allow this sect of the population to have more federal-fund-based loan and grant programs.

Tribal Colleges

Native Americans were never prohibited from attending colleges or universities. Their struggle was more of being recognized than being accepted. Tribal students' enrollment has been minimal for years. As a result of extreme racism and marginalization, the Native Americans have suffered severe violence and turbulence. Tribal colleges were created as a result of the lack of access to higher education for Native Americans—in essence, they wanted higher education on their land and for their purposes, as they no longer trusted the US system. The classification of tribal college was formed by the Carnegie Foundation and references tribal colleges that are controlled and located on reservations.

Questions

1. How can tribal colleges be successful?
2. How can students at tribal colleges thrive?
3. As a student, reflect on some problems you have overcome. Do they relate to the Native Americans' problems?
4. As a professor/teacher/student, how can you help Native Americans persevere in their studies?

Purpose of Education

If several college dropouts have attained millionaire status, why is it important or even relevant for people to complete high school and attend college? If a person can work hard and gain a better life, is there a need for education? Yes! Often the genius who cannot remain in school is far too bright or far too ahead of the natural course of thinking that they can no longer contain their natural ability. Sadly, that does not apply to the vast majority. In America, education is the great equalizer.

As an equalizer, there are several aspects of greatness and purpose. In that, the purpose of education is to create and establish utility and culture. Creating utility, the education system creates students who are useful and skillful. Once students have graduated, they can perform a service or add to society in its labor force. Creating culture, on the other hand, is developing the student to understand aspects of information from all angles. Hopefully, learning in the K–20 environment will aid in making students efficient and skillful, and provide a pathway to goal achievement and attainment. Education is supposed to create brilliant minds that will critically challenge social ills. These thinkers will develop pathways and gateways for others.

The list demonstrate the various purposes for education:

Literate	Learning society; critical thinkers
Democracy	Developed citizens Social skills Occupational preparations
Development	Orderly citizens evolve into sequential members of society Personal growth and development Fullest realization of what it is to be a human being Morally apt citizen Creative citizen Productive citizen Assimilation of immigrants

Questions

1. According to the table, are schools currently preparing students to be morally apt? Creative? Productive? If so, how? If not, explain.
2. Why is it important to have immigrants assimilate to American culture?

Current State of Education

America, known as the richest land in the world, has several issues. One issue is the state of American education. States are reducing funding to public schools, and vouchers are being extended to poor families to attend private or better performing schools. Common Core has taken precedence in several states—and others rejected it. Few people know what a "good" or "sound" education is—leaving educators grasping at straws. Curricula changes every two to three years—when real data are usually compiled over at least five years. Teaching, the career that launches all others, offers the lowest pay. When I taught, janitors made more than first-year teachers did.

References

American Council on Education (2006). Minorities in higher education: Twenty-second annual status report. Retrieved March 18, 2013 from http:www.acenet.educa/Content/NavigationMenu/About AnnualReport/ACEAR05web.pdf.

Brubacher, J. S. & Rudy, W. (1976). Higher education in transition: A history of American colleges and universities. 1636-1976. New York, NY: Harper & Row.

Codding, J. B. & Rothman, R, & Tucker, M.S. (1999). *The new American high school: Educating for the 21st century*. Newberry Park, CA: Corwin.

Lucas, C.J. (2006). *American higher education*. New York: Palgrave Macmillan.

Lazerson, M. (1998). *Discontent in the field of dreams: American higher education*, 1945-1990. (Report No. NCPI-3-01). Stanford, CA: National Center for Postsecondary Improvement. (ERIC Document Reproduction Service No. ED428588).

Manno, B.V. (1995). In the image of the great society: Reinventing k–12 education in the Clinton administration. Indianapolis, IN: Hudson Institute.

MacLaurin v. Oklahoma State Regents for Higher Education, 339 U. S. (1950).

National Center for Education Statistics. Urban Schools. The Challenge of Location and Poverty. Retrieved: December 30, 2008, from: Institute of Educational Sciences: http:nces.ed.gov/pubs/web /9618ex.asp

Sweatt v. Painter, 339 U.S. 629 (1950).

Thomas, B. (1997). *Plessy v. Ferguson: A brief history without documents*. Boston: Bedford Books.

CHAPTER TWO

THE REFORM MOVEMENT

Introduction

The Reform Movement is critical in American education. Imagine using a wheelchair and not being able to attend school, or being blind and having nowhere to learn. The Reform Movement is connected to Civil Rights. This movement in particular sought to re-tool and create best practices centered on inclusion: who, what, why, and how to create an environment where learning is paramount and all students feel successful. Most reforms in this chapter reflect federal mandates. As the history shows, the focus shifts to understanding the impact of immigrants in education and the need to become more diverse. This diversity has been called and named several things; the one that has been more pervasive is Culturally Relevant Teaching. This chapter focuses on the need for and possible impacts of the theory. As you read, think about and question why so many outside the profession of education want to govern its practices.

Americans in the 1950s were becoming better educated and students across the nation were completing high school at higher rates. On the other hand, sparked by several unexpected incidents, the question of whether the schools were providing adequate education was at the forefront of educational policy writers. These debates brought about questions of whether regulatory mechanisms existed (racism) to ensure the different educational systems were delivering the best quality education to students.

One of the critical occurrences, the launching of the Russian satellite Sputnik in 1957, rocked American education to its core. This caused several to openly criticize the educational system for failing to provide students with sufficient teaching in basic skills, especially in the areas of math and science. In 1958, as a result of the Russians' scientific advantage, Americans passed the National Defense Education Act (NDEA). The NDEA provided federal aid to all levels of education in the United States, including public and private institutions (Barrett, 2005). NDEA paid for academic equipment and encouraged students to pursue study in the fields of math and science. Using NDEA, school districts were held accountable for creating more rigorous curricula, upgrading teaching materials, and adding the required instruments for math and science. Slowly, high schools began to provide students with improved instruction.

Despite the efforts, America fell short in accomplishing its objective of having an elite world status in math and science. Bunting (1999) states, "there was no direct evidence that students had learned more, or that society was any better served, as a consequence of the redoubled foci on academics. There was, in fact, a strong suspicion that the foundation of education had been narrowly drawn, in that other important goals had been sacrificed in the quest for excellence" (p. 213).

At the same time, society had grown tired waiting for a moral and ethical resolution to the segregation and unequal education practices. African Americans demanded rights in education. On May 17, 1954, the United States Supreme Court decided on behalf of Oliver Brown against the school board of Topeka, Kansas, and stated that having separate schools for African Americans and whites was unequal. This ruling outlawed racial segregation within public education facilities. The law stated separate-but-equal could never provide African Americans with facilities of the same standards as were available to whites. During this ruling, Americans did not embrace multiculturalism or integration. Americans, per the law, had to improve equity within schools. This decision created a set of challenges and actions that are still relevant in public education today (Eaton, 2007). Early, the challenge was how to desegregate schools without violence. After the turbulent attempts to desegregate schools in the 1950s and 1960s, the challenges turned to how to make the curriculum more ethnically balanced. Banks (2005) said early efforts to integrate diverse ethnic groups into the curriculum were hasty. In addition to demanding diverse cultures be represented in curricula, African American groups also pressured school districts to hire teachers of color and to include diversity in all district decision-making bodies. During the 1960s, African Americans and justice-minded whites sought to end discrimination in public places and institutions such as education and public housing. This cultural upheaval engendered a reform movement in education, called multicultural education. The term "multicultural" is used to extend the notion beyond African Americans and whites to include Latinos, Cubans, and Asian Americans, students with disabilities, Native Americans, and now, LBGT.

Banks (2005) defines multicultural education as a concept, a process, and an educational reform movement. Beginning in the 1960s and continuing to the present day, it is known that students who look like and are raised in environments similar to their white teachers do better in public school than others do. Education professional call this disparity the achievement gap. Multicultural education, as a reform, seeks to address the problems inherent in minority student achievement.

Education theorists have defined the concept of differentiation as providing a diverse group of students with multiple options to process information and to demonstrate their learning on the same topic and in the same class (Tomlinson, 2000; Hall, 2002). Differentiation in teaching and learning grew out of the need for school districts to accommodate students with disabilities. The Education for All Handicapped Children Act of 1975, Pub.L.94-142, stimulated the growth of multicultural education because of federal power, in the form of funding, mandated differentiation for disabled students.

Questions

1. What are the far-reaching implications of this section? Why?
2. Should schools be racially balanced?
3. Should schools have access and equity for all students? Why or why not?

Before Bush's No Child Left Behind Act attempted to reform urban education, Reagan, in the 1980s, created the National Commission on Excellence in Education (NCEE). NCEE criticized the public education system for being dysfunctional. Their report, "A Nation at Risk," highlighted that overall student assessments were low. The commission determined that students were lazy and unengaged, and as a result were responsible for public education's lack of productivity. In addition, the report asserted that schools were sub-par because teachers were poorly qualified. Fearing a rising tide of mediocrity that they thought threatened the economic well-being of the nation, the government pressured schools to increase their standards, and passed laws designed to make licensing for teachers and administrators more difficult (Kowalaski, 2005).

"A Nation at Risk" was a proposed reformation based on the development of standards-based curricula to improve student learning. To create and improve the educational system, the NCEE made several recommendations, which included enhancing language arts, science and math curricula, extended school day and year, and programs that better prepared teachers to perform their duties.

While the report was widely accepted, several flaws emerged. The analysis of achievement, the positive trends in achievement among disadvantaged students, was completely overlooked (Guthrie & Springer, 2004). In spite of that, the report drew widespread attention and created a national discussion about education reform that led to testing and accountability practices that are still practiced and prevalent today. Currently, there is compelling evidence that the education system in America remains outdated and the documented concerns remain very relevant.

Clinton

In 1992, President Bill Clinton made an attempt to reform education. In response to the concerns documented in "A Nation at Risk," as well as those from other sources, on March 31, 1994, President Clinton signed into law Goals 2000: Educate America Act. This act introduced the idea of curriculum standards as a key of the reform movement. The president intended the following goals of ensuring all children will start school ready to learn; increasing the high school graduation rate; improving learning by establishing challenging academic standards for all students, particularly in math and science; and making schools safe and drug free (Manno, 1995).

Questions

1. Did schools get better or worse while Clinton was in office?
2. As we review the drug laws of the 1990s, were children safer in school or at home?
3. Were the Goals 2000 ever reached?

This legislation sought to have states focus more on the outcomes of district and school efforts and less on compliance with rules and regulations. States were encouraged to develop content and performance standards in core subject areas and to align their entire educational systems, including assessment, curriculum, instruction, professional development, and parental and community involvement with standards (Puma, Raphael, Olson, & Hannaway, 2000). While these goals were sensible, the reality of attaining the goals was thwarted by their overly ambitious nature and a failure of federal funding. Critics felt these concepts were too restrictive and imposed a set of uniform standards.

Bush

Each reform seeks to make education better, particularly for people who are disadvantaged. Reforms are often intended to improve the education of students who are in lower socioeconomic status ranks. No Child Left Behind is no different. Its purpose was to improve local standards in the areas of complacency, special education, and increasing the use of data to drive instruction. NCLB also wanted to improve the quality of education by improving performance, improving instruction by using research-based practices, increasing and creating parental programs, professional development, reinvesting in early literacy, and creating an emphasis of core academic subjects. In addition, in its inception in 2001, NCLB recreated Title I funding to schools and mandated a standards-based curriculum. States were to develop standards and give specific tests to receive funding.

NCLB focused on basic skills and attempted to level the field for all students' learning. Standardized tests were to be given to all students under the same conditions. Schools receiving Title I funding must meet Adequate Yearly Progress. NCLB Act required schools to:

- Develop Adequate Yearly Progress (AYP) statewide measurable objectives; these objectives must be met in all sub-categories
- Goal of having 100% proficiency within twelve years
- AYP is based on benchmark (mid-quarter tests) and end-of-year state tests
- Ninety-five percent of each group and sub-group must participate
- Must have at least three years of data

All teachers, according to NCLB Act, must be highly qualified. The highly qualified status is determined by each state. As a teacher, the states I worked in required a college degree with a major or minor in the field. In addition to having highly qualified teachers, the act also required states to inform military recruiters to have contact information and access to the student if that information were shared with universities or employers. Students could opt out of allowing this information to be shared.

If schools did not meet AYP, the following steps were taken:

- Two years of low performance: schools would be labeled "In need of Improvement" and required to develop a two-year developmental plan. Students are given the option to transfer to a better or higher-performing school.
- Three years of low performance: schools are forced to provide free tutoring and supplemental education services to struggling students.

- Four years of low performance: school is placed in "Corrective Action." In this phase, the staff is replaced, new curriculum is used, and longer school days and/or longer time in class are implemented.
- Five years of low performance: forces schools to restructure entire school; possibly becoming a charter school or hiring a private company to oversee the management of the school.

Strengths of NCLB

- Increased accountability of schools and teachers
- Linked standards to outcomes
- Gave parents information on teacher and school status
- Provided foundations for parental involvement
- Provided safe harbor
- Improved test scores

Areas of concern

- Funding stopped; in some cases was not available
- Targeted for poor children
- Too much testing
- Market-based solutions
- Overall, NCLB opened the door to use standardized testing to validate teachers and students. Its intentions appeared to be good; however, market-based solutions seem too capitalistic a concept for educational leaders.

Questions

1. Did No Child Left Behind reach its target goals?
2. As a result of No Child Left Behind, how did education become better? Worse?
3. Review the tenets of No Child Left Behind; why was it targeted for poor and disadvantaged children?
4. What are some risk factors in allowing market-based solutions in education?

Obama

Race to the Top (RTTT or R2T) is a $435 billion contest for education innovation and reform in state and local K–12 education. RTTT has been funded by the American Recovery and Reinvestment Act of 2009. Points are awarded on this by performance-based standards, compliance with Common Core, providing more access to charter schools, turning around low-performing schools, and creating data systems. Race to the Top was created to strengthen four key areas of education: development of rigorous standards and better assessments; adoption of better data systems to provide schools, teachers, and parents with information about student success; support for teachers and school leaders to become more effective; and increased emphasis and resources for the rigorous interventions needed to turn around lowest-performing schools. To gain RTTP funding, school districts had to follow a structured system and were awarded points in specific categories. The point system for funding is composed of:

- Great teachers and leaders (138 points)
- Improving teacher and principal effectiveness based on performance (58)
- Providing high-quality pathways for aspiring teachers and principals (25)
- Providing effective support to teachers and principals (20)
- Improving the effectiveness of teacher and principal preparation programs (14)
- State success factors (125 points)
- Articulating state's education reform agenda and LEAs participation (65)
- Building strong statewide capacity to implement, scale up, and sustain proposed plans (30)
- Demonstrating significant progress in raising achievement and closing gaps (30)
- Standards and assessments (70 points)
- Developing and adopting common standards (40)

(Continued)

Race to the Top Results

State	Round 1 Score (Place)	Round 1 Result	Round 2 Score (Place)	Round 2 Result	Round 3 Score	Round 3 Result
Alabama	291.2 (37th)	–	212.0 (36th)	–	–	–
Arizona	240.2 (40th)	–	435.4 (12th)	Finalist	–	Awarded $25 million
Arkansas	394.4 (17th)	–	389.2 (21st)	–		
California	336.8 (27th)	–	423.6 (16th)	Finalist		
Colorado	409.6 (14th)	Finalist	420.2 (17th)	Finalist	–	Awarded $18 million
Connecticut	344.6 (25th)	–	379.0 (25th)	–		
Delaware	454.6 (1st)	Awarded $100 million	–	–		
District of Columbia	402.4 (16th)	Finalist	450.0 (6th)	Awarded $75 million		
Florida	431.4 (4th)	Finalist	452.4 (4th)	Awarded $700 million		
Georgia	433.6 (3rd)	Finalist	446.4 (8th)	Awarded $400 million		
Hawaii	364.6 (22nd)	–	462.4 (3rd)	Awarded $75 million		
Idaho	331.0 (28th)	–	Did Not Submit	–		
Illinois	423.8 (5th)	Finalist	426.6 (15th)	Finalist	–	Awarded $43 million
Indiana	355.6 (23rd)	–	Did Not Submit	–		
Iowa	346.0 (24th)	–	382.8 (22nd)	–		
Kansas	329.6 (29th)	–	Did Not Submit	–		
Kentucky	418.8 (9th)	Finalist	412.4 (19th)	Finalist	–	Awarded $17 million

Race to the Top Results

State	Round 1 Score (Place)	Round 1 Result	Round 2 Score (Place)	Round 2 Result	Round 3 Score	Round 3 Result
Louisiana	418.2 (11th)	Finalist	434.0 (13th)	Finalist	–	Awarded $17 million
Maine	Did Not Submit	–	283.4 (33rd)	–		
Maryland	Did Not Submit	–	450.0 (6th)	Awarded $250 million		
Massachusetts	411.4 (13th)	Finalist	471.0 (1st)	Awarded $250 million		
Michigan	366.2 (21st)	–	381.6 (23rd)	–		
Minnesota	375.0 (20th)	–	Did Not Submit	–		
Mississippi	Did Not Submit	–	263.4 (34th)	–		
Missouri	301.4 (33rd)	–	316.4 (30th)	–		
Montana	Did Not Submit	–	238.4 (35th)	–		
Nebraska	247.4 (39th)	–	295.8 (31st)	–		
Nevada	Did Not Submit	–	381.2 (24th)	–		
New Hampshire	271.2 (38th)	–	335.2 (29th)	–		
New Jersey	387.0 (18th)	–	437.8 (11th)	Finalist	–	Awarded $38 million
New Mexico	325.2 (30th)	–	366.2 (28th)	–		
New York	408.6 (15th)	Finalist	464.8 (2nd)	Awarded $700 million		
North Carolina	414.0 (12th)	Finalist	441.6 (9th)	Awarded $400 million		
Ohio	418.6 (10th)	Finalist	440.8 (10th)	Awarded $400 million		

(Continued)

Race to the Top Results

State	Round 1 Score (Place)	Round 1 Result	Round 2 Score (Place)	Round 2 Result	Round 3 Score	Round 3 Result
Oklahoma	294.6 (34th)	–	391.8 (20th)	–		
Oregon	292.6 (35th)	–	Did Not Submit	–		
Pennsylvania	420.0 (7th)	Finalist	417.6 (18th)	Finalist	–	Awarded $41 million
Rhode Island	419.0 (8th)	Finalist	451.2 (5th)	Awarded $75 million		
South Carolina	423.2 (6th)	Finalist	431.0 (14th)	Finalist		
South Dakota	135.8 (41st)	–	Did Not Submit	–		
Tennessee	444.2 (2nd)	Awarded $500 million	–	–		
Utah	379.4 (19th)	–	379.0 (25th)	–		
Vermont		–		–		
Virginia	324.8 (31st)	–	Did Not Submit	–		
Washington	Did Not Submit	–	290.6 (32nd)	–		
West Virginia	292.4 (36th)	–	Did Not Submit	–		
Wisconsin	341.2 (26th)	–	368.4 (27th)	–		
Wyoming	318.6 (32nd)	–	Did Not Submit	–		

Alaska, North Dakota, Texas, and Vermont did not submit Race to the Top applications for either round.

After both rounds, the Department of Education released the complete scoring of each application, with the intention of making the scoring process more transparent and helping states revise their applications to be more competitive for the second round of competition.

Round 1 (aka Phase 1) Winners were announced on March 29, 2010.[ ] Round 2 (aka Phase 2) Winners were announced on August 24, 2010.[ ] Round 3 (aka Phase 3) Winners were announced on December 23, 2011

- Supporting the transition to enhanced standards and high-quality assessments (20)
- Developing and implementing common, high-quality assessments (10)
- General selection criteria (55 points)
- Ensuring successful conditions for high-performing charters and other innovative schools (40)
- Making education funding a priority (10)
- Demonstrating other significant reform conditions (5)
- Turning around lowest-achieving schools (50)
- Intervening in the lowest-achieving schools and LEAs (10)
- Data systems to support instruction (47 points)
- Fully implementing a statewide longitudinal data system (24)
- Using data to improve instruction (18)
- Accessing and using state data (5)

Listed below are the awards granted to various states:

Currently, the strengths of Race to the Top are the funding and its innovativeness. At the print of this edition, President Barack Obama and Secretary of Education Arne Duncan are still in office. It may be too early to see patterns of strengths or weaknesses. The criticisms are similar to No Child Left Behind. Critics suggest:

- Tests scores are an inaccurate way to measure teachers
- High-stakes testing is not reliable
- Charter schools hinder public education
- Federal government is too involved in public K–12 education

Each reform made attempts to improve education in all states and localities. However, the perceived gaps remain. African American and Hispanic males lag behind their white counterparts. Female students, in every category, outpace their male counterparts. While the goals of each reform were and are sensible, the reality of attaining these goals was thwarted by their overly ambitious nature and a failure of federal funding. Critics felt these concepts were too restrictive and imposed uniform standards.

In spite of the efforts of 4 presidents to reform education, achievement gaps, inequality, and low assessment score prevail and remain the foci of several researchers, students and organizations.

Acceptance of Multicultural Programs

Multicultural programs and practices have long been created, but few were accepted; fewer put into practice. Known as programs and practices, multicultural programs usually advocate heroes and holidays, providing information on cultural artifacts into an existing curriculum (Banks, 2005). African American leaders and educational reformers have pressured the educational community to rewrite texts so they represent the achievements of minorities. Whitewashing, the making of white, is known in American history. Instead of providing factual information regarding history, people of color have been depicted as white or Anglo. This practice makes minority students feel inferior and they tend to disengage in learning. Tetrealut (2005) stated that rewriting texts to include African Americans and other minorities is important in making the curriculum "look like" the students in the classrooms. However, it has been noted that in science, art, social studies, and literature texts, African Americans and women have been included recently (Nieto, 1999; Banks, 2005).

Nieto (1999, 2000) has critiqued the acceptance of multicultural curricula in education, calling it a tolerance paradigm. Many in the field of education think the value of "tolerance learning" will assist in understanding differences. This thought process, according to Nieto (2000), is associated with multicultural education because it supports the status quo. This component makes people feel good about curricula because it skirts controversy and requires less work to implement. Real multicultural education takes time, effort, and participation from all—principals, teachers, and parents—and has to be a culture within the school. It is far more than organizing a program to recognize a specific sect or culture. It must be embedded in the practices of all learning.

Districts accept the tolerance paradigm because of legal battles fought during the civil rights and feminist movements. Ladson-Billings (1995) has reported that the American Association of Colleges for Teacher Education (AACTE) produced a directory of institutions that provide apt multicultural education in their preparatory programs for teachers. This report did not discuss the validity, content, or quality of the programs. At its conception, there were different standards for multicultural education, but in 1989, NCATE aligned all of the standards. In the twentieth century, the focus of education was still not on *all* people. The story of how America was started has been whitewashed and to a large degree, other historical facts have been, too.

Questions

1. What is the purpose of multicultural programs?

2. The reform movement is housed as a multicultural movement. Why not use African American history or other specific cultures to align with the history currently presented?
3. Why is it important to learn the true history and the history of other cultures?
4. Why is it important to understand the contributions of other cultures in American history?

An Urban Tale

As a teacher in an urban learning environment, issues of race and culture became a concern. I began to teach at FarSide Elementary Middle School in 2006. Welcoming my large classes, per the direction of school leadership, I immediately administered the reading assessment. Much to my surprise, none of the students in one class were reading at or above grade level. In fact, most were reading at third- and fourth-grade levels. Teaching these students became one of the most difficult things I had ever done. Their approach to education included a lack of participation, engagement, or trust. Even though they tried to run me away, after some time, the students began to reveal their stories about their educational experiences. Their stories were horrific. They had been a cohort, as most had been in pre-K and kindergarten together. In the first grade, this group of students were classified as bright, testing above average on required state standardized tests. In third grade, their teacher quit and there was never a permanent replacement. The students said there was no "consistent substitute teacher and they were never really taught." They chronicled having several hours of physical education, sitting in with other classes, and going to art several times daily. As they recalled that year, it became obvious they were painting a picture of dysfunction and poor administrative decisions.

In fourth grade, their pregnant teacher left in November, promising to return in January, but did not. Again they had no teacher or consistent instruction for the remainder of the year. By fifth grade, as a result of not expecting teachers to stay, they became, in the words of their principal, "the terrors of the school." Another teacher was employed, but student behaviors and attitudes toward learning forced him out. After their first quarter, another teacher was hired, but by the end of third quarter, she was found in the corner crying and repeating, "I am not afraid of these children." As these same students entered the sixth grade, their science teacher openly told the class that she was a witch and would cast spells on them if they did not do their work. They tied her up, and she left. By mid-year, they had wrapped their English teacher in a telephone cord, and their math teacher passed out on the floor after urinating on herself in front of them. In February, the assistant principal and the instructional coach took over the class and were assigned to teach these students. After all of that, these students met me.

As a class, we had to make some decisions. We discussed their education and I asked if they thought it was fair, or right, hoping they would open up to me about their educational history. They felt they had been let down by the system. They had no respect for the principal because they thought she could have better planned and prepared for all of the changes they encountered. As they continued to talk, they also described the relationships they had with their teachers. One common theme was that most students felt their teachers were racists who denigrated their current living conditions and spoke of them having dismal futures. Teachers told them they would only work at McDonald's and to remember, "I like extra ketchup with my fries." Others told them to only expect a Wal-Mart job—not in leadership—or work as mechanics and other blue-collar positions. They further explained, "When you act like animals at the zoo, you can't expect to become a world-class millionaire or citizen. The jails are waiting for you." One student, a white girl, said a teacher had an interesting conversation with her: "Why do you go to school here? Do you know you can be anything?" The student was upset because she felt all of her classmates could become successful without regard to their current situation. Moreover, the student's parents were white and Hispanic, which made the student feel the teacher was insensitive to her and lacked awareness.

Countering this, I explained that I had said some of the same things—warning them of life on welfare, their options, and other pitfalls of poverty mixed with bad decisions. "What's the difference?" I asked. Silently, they looked at me and someone found the courage to say, "You're black. Even if you ain't from here, you know. You know—and you care. When you fuss at us, it's because you care and you want what's best for us—not because you don't think we can or we won't be anything. You fuss because you want us to become more than what we are today. White teachers don't."

I was shocked.

I was hurt.

As a child, I had white teachers. They were excellent. These teachers held my hand, told me I could be anything, and made me work hard. They made my potential flourish. What happened? Had these teachers disappeared? Am I that teacher? Now that I know this behavior exists, what do I do? How do I navigate this?

As I began to think and reflect on my experiences as a teacher in urban environments, several of my students, once we had a relationship, said similar things. (I am not a great teacher. I have several flaws.) They felt their white teachers did not understand them and failed to connect with them. The students wondered why the teachers wanted to teach them, and in an urban environment. They rarely asked teachers those questions because they did not develop and had not developed a close relationship with them. I was told if the students did ask questions, it was often viewed as disrespectful and they were sent to the principal's office.

I also listened to teachers talk about their experiences in the classroom and heard comments such as: "These kids aren't going to amount to much," "It doesn't matter what I teach them, they won't be anything anyway," "They'd better build more jails because we are going to need them," and "I want extra ketchup with my fries as I drive through in my Benz." The worst comment: "I am the zookeeper and you all are the animals at the zoo—monkeys, lions, elephants: they learn better than you all." These comments haunted me and I could only imagine what they did to the children who heard them. Once uttered, the children never forgot. The students often said they did not do well because no one at school cared if they did. Hearing those comments from the teachers and the students left me wondering if white suburban teachers could be better teachers of urban students—could they be introduced to a culture of good teaching practices. If they could, then certainly I, a middle-class suburbanite, could, too.

Questions

1. What are some issues or concerns as you read about the school, teachers and students?
2. After reading this, think about your school experience. Does it mirror that of the students profiled?

While working at FarSide Elementary Middle School, it became apparent that a culture of learning had not been established. I wondered if this was pervasive in the school district. My job changed and so did my purvue of teaching and learning. As I became an administrator working with elementary schools, it became apparent that the scenario I experienced was not exclusive to FarSide. Through several observations, and encounters with teachers, I realized that teacher expectations of their students and their relationships with students may have a strong connection to the achievement of students. I became more aware of principals' concerns, too. Principals had been grappling with the same questions and attempting to train and use professional development to better position teachers to teach urban students.

A Rural Tale

I had been out of the classroom for several years. Due to lack of funding, I found myself back in a place where I really did not want to be. Despite the education and experience, I was teaching again. While I love the classroom, I am not a great teacher. And it is in a high school. I recalled my high school years—I loved my English teacher, but I also knew the students had changed since I graduated. More pervasive than anything else, in this location, I would be teaching people I had never taught before: white people. Could I reach them? Or … .

I entered the class, had lesson plans, and met the teachers. Some young, some old, some black, some white. What was amazing to me was many of the teachers had actually gone to school there. Their memories of the school were quite different than its current reality. The alumni teachers went to the school when it was segregated. Even after integration, because of the scarcity of minorities, few ever went to the school.

Over the past ten to fifteen years, the school had become a vast majority of minorities. African Americans moved into the area and some were bussed from the "inner city," several Hispanics and a large population of Arab and Vietnamese people had moved into the surrounding area. Test scores were borderline, morale was low, and students were defiant. While they were students who would test the boundaries, they were not bad kids. Looking at the raw data, students were barely missing the targeted benchmark scores. Unlike the alumni teachers' memories, this "new" school was different. And they complained. Loudly. The students could feel the teachers' disdain. Some acted out in specific teachers' classes, others roamed the halls, while others sat in class and refused to engage.

I was hired to remediate. I walked into a classroom of minority boys. The boys ranged in age and classification. Because they had not passed the ninth-grade end-of-year test, they were still classified as freshmen. Imagine being 16, 18, or even 19 and still a freshman. I had one girl in the class. As I began to teach them, I realized what I had heard about them was not true. The data reflected students who did not read at grade level, who did not comprehend above fourth-grade level, and who were very difficult to teach, as their behavior ranged from nice to nasty to vicious. Admittedly, I was intimidated.

As I began to talk and work with other teachers, I heard their voices about the students. "These are throwaway kids." "Oh, her parents care about her … they went to the museum." "Oh, that one, he has good parents, but … he is too busy trying to get jumped into a gang than really being focused on school." And, "Sometimes I feel like I am at the zoo." Not again!

Again, I was with students nobody wanted and few cared about. Again, I started not with relationship building, but with really giving them work they could do. I gave them worksheets of grammar. They hated it. When I graded it, they loved it. Most had never been given positive feedback from a teacher. One student said "It's been so long since I got an A, I didn't know I could." The walls began to crumble and the relationships began to form. The class was small—we had great days, we had awful days, we had trying days, but in the end, we had success. In December, of the fourteen students, ten passed the test on the first try, one had to retake the test, and I am not sure what happened to the others. They were happy. I even got hugs.

But the fourteen students struggled in other classes. Their behavior was different. The effort they gave me was nonexistent in other classes. When I asked why or confronted them, they said, "She doesn't care about me." My heart broke again.

Two Schools

These two schools, one urban, the other rural, located in different states, had the same pervasive energy. Failure. Both schools face extreme disparities and problems centered on expectations, class, and culture. Each school had an especially long history of failure, of problematic students, teachers, and an environment that did not promote high expectations. The urban school is located in a historic community, once known for hosting legendary African American singers and concerts, and being critical to the Civil Rights Movement. Now, the same community is notorious for its open-air drug market, prostitution, public housing projects, and ghettos. It is widely known that if anyone wants something illegal, it can be found in this community. While there is a strong police presence in the area, there are few arrests or negative repercussions for persons who break the law. Parents in this community belong to gangs, openly fight to protect their cliques, and seem to teach their practices to their children. Allegiance and loyalty are the mainstay of the neighborhoods. The children bring that culture and mentality into the school; one result being brutal fighting within the learning environment.

The rural school is known for having its own culture and identity. They liked being rural and a farm country—it is a community, like the urban school, where generations attended the school. While they did not actively fight the influx of African American and Hispanic students, they were not too happy. There is a silent divide. If students had not been born in or around the area, and in the same tracking area of schools, they were outsiders. Teachers had never changed their approach to education, teaching, and learning. This school had its elite, rich white students whose parents were members of the Ku Klux Klan. This school had its middle-class students whose parents were very concerned about their children, but the parents never came to school. This school had the abject poor students—some land-rich, but socioeconomically struggling. In this dynamic, few lines were ever crossed. Students found unique pockets of friendship and sat in clusters in the cafeteria. While bullying was not a problem, sex and fighting were. Students were open about having sex, but in secret locations. And students would plan to fight in school.

Both schools over the last three years reported more than eighty suspensions. In the urban environment, one hundred percent of the students were on FARMS (free and reduced lunch), while only seventy-five percent were at the rural school. In the urban setting, students freely ate lunch and talked among their friends. But in the rural environment, students who received FARMS would not eat. If they did eat, they would be first or last in line because they did not want anyone to know they received free lunch. The attendance for each school ranged at about eighty percent daily, while the thrust and district requirement is ninety-five percent. Students in the urban environment were highly transient, meaning they would move from school to school. The rural school was quite different. The students came and stayed.

In both places, as teachers and principals began to make connections and build relationships with students and parents, they began to recognize that most fathers were not in the home; over eighty-five percent in the urban community and thirty-five percent in the rural community were incarcerated. Few books were in the home in the urban community. While the rural community had more books, in the lower socioeconomic homes, few ever read the books. Few had technology. In both communities, a disproportionate number of students were in group homes, being raised by grandparents, or cluster families. In the urban environment, the single grandmother was responsible for raising her grandchildren because their fathers were in jail and the mothers were strung out. In each school, at least ten percent of the population was homeless. In each setting, they did not trust outsiders. Students in each setting questioned the necessity of the education they were receiving and most were afraid they were going to become exactly what their parents were.

Questions

1. What are some issues that stand out at the urban school?
2. What are some issues that stand out at the rural school?
3. How are the two schools alike? How are they different?
4. As a principal, how would you approach each school?
5. As a parent, how do you approach and prepare your child for either school?
6. As a teacher, how do you prepare to teach in either school?

Urban education has become the focal point of scrutiny as people investigate academic achievement and how schools in urban areas create their learning environment. As I found myself in both urban and rural, I wondered why no one focused on the rural environment. It too has its social ills. At each school setting, students were very honest in revealing their perceived realities of education. The groups of students I encountered were bright, but they felt education had failed them due to lack of planning, lack of teacher connection, and overly lecture-styled learning environments. Knowing their teachers had low expectations, or perhaps no expectations of them, students often complied with the beliefs of their teachers. Attempting to reverse examples of psychological damage and apathetic toward learning (as learned behavior), knowledge was sought to answer these questions:

- Why are students feeling apathetic about learning?
- What can be done to increase student engagement?
- How can teachers' perceptions be changed toward students of lower socioeconomic backgrounds? Minorities?

These are difficult questions and may never be answered correctly. Everyone keeps saying this is not about race. Everyone keeps saying this is more about socioeconomic status. It is about race. It is also about class. If we were to unfold the dynamic of poverty, we would see not just minorities, but all races and cultures represented.

Years ago, schools did not focus on educating all children. Teachers concentrated on the good students. These students were classified as good if they paid attention in class, followed directions, did their assigned work, completed reports on time, and scored well on tests. The emergence of urban and rural education environments brought several challenges. In each setting, research shows skill-set decline and how student–teacher relationships impact student academic success. There are few surprises about each environment—poverty, racism, and unequal academic achievement are common. As a result of socioeconomic differences, students and teachers often enter the classroom with different ideals and expectations. It has been noted that a solid academic core is most important for all students, especially rural and urban students, as college preparation is eminent in this competitive global society (Bottoms, Han, & Presson, 2005) has changed. This change has brought several challenges.

Overcoming these challenges, teachers, principals, and the culture of the school must be changed. These changes can be mitigated by incorporating the tenets of culturally mediated instruction and culturally relevant teaching. Culturally Mediated Instruction came about as a result of a multicultural influx of the 1980s. In its origins, culturally mediated instruction is deeply connected to multicultural education. Multicultural education is defined as a concept, a process, and an educational reform movement (Banks, 2005). Other terms synonymous with culturally mediated instruction, according to Delpit (1995), are, "culturally appropriate instruction, culturally congruent, and culturally responsive." (p. 97). Gay (2000) includes the terms "culturally relevant, sensitive centered, congruent, reflective, mediated, contextualized, synchronized and responsive" (p. 27). Developed with an understanding of the cultural reform movement, culturally mediated instruction is a way of teaching that is inclusive and sensitive. Instruction or teaching can be classified as culturally mediated when diverse methods of knowing, understanding, and presenting information are incorporated into the learning process. Gay (2000) defines culturally mediated instruction as using knowledge, prior experiences, frames of reference, and performance styles of ethnically diverse students to make learning encounters more relevant to and effective for them. According to Ladson-Billings (1994), this level of teaching should occur in an environment that supports multicultural outlooks while allowing for inclusion of knowledge that is relevant to students. Creating this environment, a teacher must demonstrate what Gay (2000) outlines as the six characteristics of culturally mediated instruction: validating, comprehensive, multidimensional, empowering, transformative, and emancipatory.

Culturally Relevant Teaching

Coining the phrase in 1997, Gloria Ladson-Billings created a revolutionary style and method of teaching inclusive to brown and black children—or children who felt left out. American schools will allow any student to enter, often those who enter are not truly educated. Marginalized students often act out, become dismissive, rebel, or check out mentally of the thinking, learning, and education process. Once turned off, students are *referred* (as tracking is no longer a strategy) into Special Education programs. Offering several strategies, the core element is to expose teachers to a style that displays cultural competence; which is a skill at teaching cross-cultural or multi-cultural concepts. This form of teaching creates an empowering learning environment where students can grow daily. The principles of Culturally Relevant Teaching are:

- **Identity development**—teachers are true and comfortable with themselves; teach within their identity and because of their own self comfort, seek to make connections with students
- **Equity and Excellence**—teacher work to ensure multicultural content is used with the prescribed curriculum content. Additionally, teachers recognize the relationship with students and work to create equal access to learning and have high expectations of all students.

- **Developmental Appropriateness**—teachers work to provide variations of learning and teaching styles. As a teacher/professor, I train future teachers to be prepared to teach a concept three different ways so students who learn in modalities other than lecture, can grasp the concept.
- **Teaching the Whole Child**—as teachers, it is important to understand the entire child. This does not mean reading his file and holding past transgressions against the child, but understanding the context of how the child sees the world. To do this, teachers must seek to know the socio-cultural aspect of the child … without bias. In this context, teachers can better understand why and how the child behaves and responds in a certain manner. This also gives a bird's eye view into the how to approach the child when attempting to teach and build relationships.
- **Student Teacher Relationships**—Teachers must make the child understand their best interest is at heart. This does not suggest being a push over or fearing the child, but understanding how to motivate, how to provide personal care and remaining vigilant in difficult times.
- **Manage Student Emotions**—Adult learners are often left out of the model when discussing learning. However, in this, adults are paramount. Teachers must understand adults come to the class with their own set of ideals and expertise. Educators must recognize and respect this aspect of adult and often high school learners. When emotions erupt in the course, allow the positive emotions to be released. When the emotions are negative, create a learning and teachable moment so students can understand how to deal with their variations of emotions.

Validating

Teaching is validating when teachers teach through the strengths of the students. Gay (2000) explains validation occurs through teachers legitimizing cultural heritages of different groups, bridging meaningfulness between home and school experiences, the using of a variety of instructional strategies that connect to students' learning styles, teaching praise of others' work, and incorporating multicultural information and resources.

Comprehensive

The teacher attempts to teach the whole child. In teaching the whole child, teachers become mediators, consultants, and advocates to assist with the connection of culture to education (Ladson-Billings, 1994). Education designed to address students of color incorporates culturally mediated instruction that adds value to the curriculum.

Multidimensional

Culturally meditated instruction encompasses curriculum content, learning context, classroom climate, student teacher relationships, instructional techniques, and performance assessments (Gay, 2000). Students in a multidimensional classroom are learning and critically thinking. Their individual needs are being met.

Empowering

Empowering students is easy on the surface, but true empowerment takes time. This approach enables a student to become a better human being and a more successful learner. This is translated into confidence, courage, competence, and the will to act. Teachers must demonstrate their level of expectancy of success to their students and show them how to succeed.

Transformative

Culturally responsive teaching does not incorporate traditional educational practices with respect to students of color (Gay, 2000). This allows teachers to respect and learn the cultures and experiences of various groups and then use information gained to build relationships that lead to resources for teaching and learning. It appreciates the existing strengths and accomplishments of all students and develops them further in instruction. The verbal creativity and story-telling that is unique among some African Americans in informal social interactions is acknowledged as a gift and contribution and used to teach writing skills. Other ethnic groups prefer to study together in small groups. When teachers are transformative, often more opportunities for them and other students to participate in cooperative learning can be provided in the classroom. Banks (1991) asserts that if education is to empower marginalized groups, it must be transformative. Being transformative involves helping "students to develop the knowledge, skills, and values needed to become social critics who can make reflective decisions and implement their decisions in effective personal, social, political, and economic action" (p. 131).

Emancipatory

Emancipatory practices in the culturally mediated classroom lift the veil of presumed absolute authority from conceptions of scholarly truth typically taught in schools (Gay, 2003, p. 35). This forces teachers to reveal their weaknesses and acknowledge that students have prior knowledge. This is done to uncover student interest in concepts and create learning about those concepts.

References

Banks, J. (2004). Multicultural Education: Historical development dimensions. In Banks, J.A. & Banks, C.A. (Eds.). (2004). Handbook on research multicultural education (2nd ed). San Francisco, CA: Jossey Bass.

Banks, J.A. & Banks, C.A. (Eds). (2004). Handbook on research multicultural education. (2nd ed). San Francisco, CA: Jossey Bass.

Brown v. Board of Education of Topeka 347 U.S. (1954).

Delpit, L. (1995, 2006). Other people's children: cultural conflict in the classroom. New York, NY: The New Press.

Delpit, L., & Kilgour Dowdy, J. (2002). The skin that we speak: thoughts on language and culture in the classroom. New York: The New Press.

Gay, G. (2004). Curriculum theory and multicultural education, In Banks, J.A. & Banks, C.A. (Eds). (2004). *Handbook of Research in Multicultural Education*. San Francisco, CA: Jossey Bass.

Gay, G. (2003). *The importance of multicultural education*. Educational Leadership, 61(4), 30–35.

Gay, G. (2000). Culturally responsive teaching: Theory, research, and practice. New York: Teachers College Press.

Gay, G. (1997). Multicultural infusion in teacher education: Foundations and applications. Peabody Journal of Education, 72, 150–177.

Gay, G. (1994). Beyond Brown: Promoting equality through multicultural education. *Journal of Curriculum and Supervision*, 19(3), 193–216.

Ladson-Billings, G. (1994). The dreamkeepers: Successful teachers of African American children. San Francisco: Jossey Bass.

Ladson-Billings, G. (1995a). But that's just good teaching! The case for culturally relevant pedagogy. *Theory into Practice*, 34(3), 159–165.

Ladson-Billings, G. & Tate, W. (1995). Toward a theory of culturally relevant pedagogy. *American Educational Research Journal*, 32(3), 465–491.

Ladson-Billings, G. (1995). Social and institutional analysis toward a theory of culturally relevant pedagogy. American Educational Research Journal, Vol 32, No 3. (autumn, 1995), pp. 465–491.

Ladson-Billings, G. & Gomez, M. L. (2001). Just showing up: Supporting early literacy through teachers' professional communities. *Phi Delta Kappan*. Bloomington, Vol. 82. Page 675.

Ladson-Billings, G. (2004). New directions in multicultural education: complexities, boundaries, and critical race theory. In Banks, J.A. & Banks, C.A. (Eds). Handbook of Research Multicultural education. San Francisco: Jossey Bass.

Ladson-Billings, G. (2005). The evolving role of critical race theory in educational scholarship. Ethnicity and Education, 8(1), 115–119.

CHAPTER THREE

TEACHERS

Introduction

Teachers are the crux of the matter. If students do well, they are the hero. If students fail, they are the villain. If students have high attendance, it is a result of the teacher's engaging lessons and teaching practices, but if students skip class or rarely come to school, the cause is the teacher is boring or lacks engaging lesson plans. As education has changed to become better, the role of the teacher has changed. Culturally Relevant Teaching and Culturally Mediated Instruction are concepts created and practiced by educators. Gay and Ladson-Billings are the founders of this style of teaching. They have done it. They have taught people how to implement the practice successfully in their learning environments. Initially, the practice is difficult, cumbersome, because it is not natural. My education was whitewashed. As I taught, I saw my students' education was whitewashed, too. This chapter is dedicated to unpacking the practice and theory to ensure teachers and students everywhere are taught—not tracked—like the student in the introduction.

The Role of the Teacher

Teaching is a rewarding profession. The rewards come when least expected, and often once a teacher sees a student progress over the year, it makes the pain and the development of the student all worthwhile. Teachers must keep in the forefront of their minds why they are teaching. Do you really love children? If not, do not enter the classroom. Do you really want to create a better tomorrow by informing and transforming the ideology of thinking? If not, do not enter the classroom. Have you been laid off and are seeking a job that pays the bills? Do not enter teaching. With the economic stress and corporate downsizing, several are seeking to teach. Many think because they have a degree, they can teach. It is not true. If you have not been trained, if you are not interested in attaining certification, if you are not interested in investing time and effort into children, please do not enter the classroom. If you are making an attempt to save children from their situation, do not enter the classroom. In this mindset, the decisions adults make are based on their past, their presumptions, and how they think the child should live, grow, and develop. As a teacher, your focus is on emotional and academic development. You are not to guide the child into a career path or a life. Just because the path is taken by several, it does not mean it is to be the model for all.

Teach because it renews your spirit. Teach because it is impactful. No one teaches for the money. Teach for the rewards and the chance, every single day, to improve the academic outlook of the students. Teachers are not there to rescue or say, "This is all they can or will be."

Approach to Classroom Environment

Early years of teaching provide excitement and over-planning for the decoration of the classroom and learning environment. Teachers often go to specific stores seeking posters with messages. But has any consideration been given to how those messages impact students in the learning environment? Often, the answer is no. As a former teacher, I created bulletin boards, but left them blank until I met my students. If I taught African Americans, it would be insensitive to create walls with other cultures and leave them out.

The learning environment must be engaging; a place students do not want to leave. How is that created? It depends on each grade level. The purpose of the exercises in this chapter is to move beyond programs for cultural relevance to make the theory and practice a function and strategy of daily teaching habits.

Before students enter the classroom, teachers already know several things about each student. "Problem students" have been identified by speaking to other teachers, students with Individual Lesson Plans (IEP) have been discussed, students who have anger management or any other problem have been reviewed by the teacher. The power a teacher has in those moments is critical. The moment a teacher reads and reviews a student's file, the teacher can make a decision—to accept the child and their past or to stereotype the child. When reading files, ask yourself:

- Why has the child been a behavior problem?
- What did past teachers/administrators do to combat the problem?
- Is the problem being addressed correctly? If not, why?
- What can you do differently to ensure the student gets your best, and the education they deserve?

Students come with several problems, issues, and concerns—but so do adults. As the adult and professional, the teacher determines the destiny of the student. Will you become a teacher who:

- Is known for referring students
- Is known for caring for students
- Is known for making predetermined statements and treatments of the student before meeting him/her?

It is very easy to refer a student and not deal with the issue. It is very easy to create a paper trail of the negative behavior of the student. Teaching transforms lives—and not just lives of good or obedient children. Using the strategies of Culturally Relevant Teaching and Culturally Mediated Instruction forces teachers to review and reflect daily on their practice.

Elementary

The environment may need to be bright, with an identified reading area. In the reading area, create posters for writing standards, reading standards, and selecting books for their level of reading. Instructions for how to treat each area is important, too. When students enter the first day, explain and role-play the expectations for each area.

The posters may need to read, "letters make words, words make sentences, sentences make paragraphs" and "How to select a book: A too-easy book is ... A too-hard book is ... A just-right book is ... . And describe the process for selecting a book. In the learning environment's library, there should be books on specific people and places that allow learners to ask questions, grow, and develop.

Using the constructs of CMI and CRT:

Validating—knowing the background of children is great, unless used against them. To validate students and create relationships, have a one-to-one conference. Use the conference to get to know students and their likes. Even five-year-olds can tell you what they like. In that discovery, plan how to teach them, plan how to make each student feel good, and show them that school is a place of respect and great learning.

Create groups and levels of students. Code them according to color or according to safari animals. Use a theme for the learning environment that is cultural and inviting. In elementary school, groups of four work best. The groups have different work—they may not read the same story, but they can read similar stories. If they must read the same story, provide different questions for each group. The higher the reading levels, the more difficult the questions.

This can be done in every subject, every day. In creating relationships with students, establish a discipline model and stick to it. Create a reward system. If Friday is "Fun Day," the students are given a specific amount of time to play and compete, and the teacher should be a part of that playing and competition. Doing this, you get to know the students and see how they function in different settings. Games allow students to use their own strategies to win.

Playing with children, having conferences, and keeping an open communication with parents validates children and allows the teacher to see the individual styles of their students, which creates a better platform for teaching to specific needs and styles of students.

Comprehensive—when learning is comprehensive, a bond of trust has been created. Teachers and students are an extended family. In this relationship, students and teachers hold each other accountable. In all aspects of learning—social, emotional, and intellectual—both parties are Socratic. Teachers train students how to ask and answer questions. As students in elementary school grow and develop, teachers can present the class with a cultural/world/state/city/neighborhood problem. The class has to collectively solve the problem. When reading, students are taught which questions to ask that probe deeper into the meaning of the text. This will teach critical-thinking skills early and allow the reader to see and understand the injustice or the problem through several lenses.

Multidimensional—akin to validating, multidimensional is creating paths for different levels of thinking. If a student does not agree with you or presents a different example, do not reject it. Instead, allow the student, within reason, to share and develop his idea. Multidimensional requires the teacher to differentiate instruction. Teachers, in planning, should create three different ways to teach a concept for the different learning styles of their students. In planning, teachers usually rely on lecture. While lecture is not as effective, it may be needed to establish the lesson. As the lesson develops, technology—listening to tapes, watching movie clips, and creating projects (allowing students to work with their hands) will engage all students.

Empowering—the learning environment needs to welcome all students. In speaking about culture, often the discussion centers on race or class. True inclusion speaks to all people. If students are in Special Education, they should not feel out of place in the classroom. Students with disabilities should be reflected, too—even if they are not *in* the classroom. In making students feel empowered, teachers can consider the following:

- Give the students something they can do well
- Speak and provide eye contact to each student entering and leaving
- Display student work—even if it is not great
- Allow students to have decision-making power
- Allow students to have a voice
- Debates
- Discussions about ideas/concepts/and issues that plague places they know and don't know

Transformative—the learning environment must be challenging and allow students to change, grow, and develop. First, the teacher must be comfortable with him- or herself. Teachers should practice being reflective and answer honestly. In the Bias Audit, be honest about what the biases are and create a plan to overcome them. Often, without knowing it, teachers impose their bias on the students. For example, if I do not eat beef or pork, my answers and reactions should not influence students to stop eating beef or pork. The teacher is to influence empowering transformation. Teachers can be honest with students about their biases, weaknesses, to create critical-thinking skills. Students are at the center of activities and they reflect on what was done correctly or incorrectly.

Emancipatory—recognize the strengths of the students and use them. This is beyond students helping create bulletin boards. Can students present in class? Can students assist with the development of the conversation? What can students do to propel the learning?

Middle School

Schools are very static. Often they are old buildings that have lockers, white walls, and the design has not been updated for several years. The concept of middle school is a place to house children who are in the middle—between elementary and high school. Rumors suggest this is the most difficult group of children to engage because of puberty, lack of attention span, and maturity levels. During this time, students are becoming their own person and are often emotional. Here, students learn and notice the opposite sex—and it often interrupts the academic setting. Getting middle school students to engage can be difficult. In elementary, students are still very excited and engaged; they want to learn, want to like and be liked by the teacher. Middle school offers something different.

These students are also seeking acceptance, but in a very low-key way. They want the teacher to like them, but not too much. As with elementary students, if there is a problem, usually it is not the teacher, but the environment or something happening to the child. As I share with my own students, do not take anything personally. Daily, teachers must decide how to affirm children and how these children will leave their classroom feeling validated.

High School

Often high school students have an almost adult feel. They, too, are children. Middle and high school are placed together because often the same ideology aids in their learning. As a high school teacher, I worked with low-performing students. Several had been marginalized since elementary school. Often this population is in dire need of intervention. Use of elementary and middle school strategies may be needed for the first several weeks. The key to being impactful is meeting the student where they are—not chiding them for their placement or development, but creating several venues for growth. Middle and high school approaches are usually not together, but for this instance, they may work. Teachers must determine the *how* of the approach.

Validating—again in middle school, knowing the background is great. However, it is an accumulation of facts—often written by teachers. Sometimes these teachers like the child and sometimes not. Some of the notes may be biased. As the children enter the class, get to know them as the person they are now. Often, some come making attempts to change behavior and fear the teacher knowing their past. Often in urban and rural environments, some students are very sensitive about home issues and do not want that exposed. It is imperative at this stage teachers have conferences with students. Additionally, teachers can invite students (according to their schedule) to have lunch with them. Having after-school study groups is also a great way to get to know students.

In the course of classroom delivery, if students are low performing, it is difficult to get them to complete the work. Teachers may need to have more time with the low-performing group to keep them on task. Ask their questions differently—and tier the questions. Allow students to have conversations, but keep a keen ear for what they are discussing and how to ensure they are all on task.

Comprehensive—this often comes in the second or third quarter for middle school students. If routines are established early, it can happen early. Trust is essential in being comprehensive. "Comprehensive" is holding students responsible for the work and students holding teachers accountable for learning and full-cycle teaching. If the teacher says they are going to do something, it must be done. If it is not, please refrain from stating "I'm the adult ..."; this statement puts the children down and creates friction. Be a person of your word and work toward goals. In middle school, students should be allowed to create their own rules and consequences for the class. The teacher is the facilitator and guiding the learning or the process.

Multidimensional—middle school–aged students want to voice their thoughts and opinions. While they may or may not be reading at grade level, this aspect can be fun and provide a different lens into the student. Students are older and open to participating in different activities. What activities can promote leadership, discussion, and problem solving all the while developing critical-thinking skills? In urban environments, seeking solutions to neighborhood problems may provide a voice. Allowing students to work in groups—with defined roles—will give students a way to demonstrate their abilities in another platform. As in elementary, three different strategies should be ready and used to engage the learner. In middle and high school, students are able to develop public-speaking skills. Allowing them to watch and then create a debate on a modern issue will aid in developing several skill sets. Again, in middle and high school, lecture is not effective. Instead of lecture, plan how to demonstrate the skill with

I do—show the students alone
We do—teacher and student work together
You do—students demonstrate their knowledge of the skill.

Empowering—in middle and high school, this is tricky. Students need to feel welcome and comfortable. Beyond feeling homey, the empowering environment may need to change regularly. It is difficult to demonstrate student work, but group work may be better. The empowering environment in middle and high schools will have walls that speak. A teacher colleague had scriptures posted on the wall and rotated powerful quotes. During the quarter, students would write about the author of the quote and its meaning. In the assignment, students had to connect their lives and decisions to the quote or scripture. In reflecting, students were given the opportunity to think about their past decisions and future options. This created a space for them to grow, develop, and assess themselves. Additionally, in middle and high school, empowerment comes from respecting students.

Transformative—in transformation, students must be able to make mistakes openly without feeling targeted or ostracized. Teachers must practice giving constructive feedback in front of the class and demonstrate how to do things. Students transform as a result of being prepared and working in an environment of trust.

Emancipatory—teachers have to work to understand the students. In understanding, the students' strengths are used. Students in middle and high school should be able to lead the class in discussion and other orchestrated activities. Over the course of time, students evolve into student leaders.

In every classroom, Accountable Talk guidelines can aid in creating positive discussions. Listed below are examples of how students and teachers can establish respect in the classroom and discussions protocol.

Expressing an OPINION or THOUGHT

- I believe …
- I think …
- In my opinion …
- I infer …
- Prior knowledge lets me know …

Responding to a Classmate's Thought

- I agree …
- I would like to add …
- I was thinking, what if …
- I would like to include …
- I partially agree …
- I'm not sure I agree; have you thought of it this way …

Asking for Clarification

- I do not understand, can you provide more details …
- Please repeat …

- I have a question …
- Can you give an example of …
- So, in other words, you think …

Lesson Plan Overview

Listed below are examples of middle school and high school lesson plans. The middle school lesson plans are before Common Core. The practices are to promote critical thinking while the readings are enjoyable to students. If students are not meeting the standard or not yet at standard, in the classroom the teacher can create reading or literacy circles to aid the engagement and reading development of students. Because middle and high school students do not like to detail their inabilities, the teacher has to be discreet and intentional when creating literacy or reading circles.

The classroom library needs to have a variety of reading levels. This lesson plan was used in seventh-grade English Language Arts. Because of the reading level, it could be used in the fourth or fifth grades. It can also be used for struggling readers in high school.

Parts of a Lesson Plan

The **content standard** is what the students should be able to do after the exercise.

The **motivation** is often a question that promotes thinking. It can also be an activity to engage students and prepare them for the assignment.

In each lesson plan, there should be a **differentiation** or **modification** plan to address learners who learn differently.

In each lesson plan, there should be an assessment to monitor the progress of students.

Content Standard: Introduction to Context Clues
Objective: Students will identify and explain information directly stated in the text by reading (select text) (for this plan, students read "Immigrant Kids") and deciphering words/language patterns.
Motivation: What is an immigrant? Do any of you know any immigrants?
Differentiation: Students will use different books that have various reading strategies and aids to ensure they have what is needed to develop their comprehension.

Introduction of Immigrant Kids

Questions: What is an immigrant? Do we know any? Are they different than we are? Why or why not? Explain how. Do you think their lives are any different than yours? If so, how?

What can a teacher do to empower students in this? How?
What can a teacher do to create a multidimensional context to this? How?
What can a teacher do to develop comprehension? How?
How can reading this text be transformative?
How can students learn the standard by reading this text?
While students are reading, they are seeking different types of context clues. The context clue guide is listed in the appendix.

In middle and high school, students read about Eleanor Roosevelt, Martin Luther King, Jr, and other social activists. Have students connect the similarities and differences of each leader. Discuss and explain why they were prevalent, how/why they are prevalent today, and how impactful they were in their time. This will include the use of Venn diagram, character traits chart, and a summary of each person profiled.

Character/ person	What the character says	What the character does	What the character thinks	What do others say about the character?	What are the main traits of the character?

A Synthesis Worksheet may also help with comparing ideas:

Selections

1. _____

2. _____

Important Points from Selection One	(How do these two selections add to the other? What are the similarities?)	Important Points from Selection Two

Write a summary of the information below.

Independent Reading Critical Analysis

This assignment allows students to self-select a book with the guidance of a librarian or teacher.

Students must select a book to critique. Student must use original sources—the use of Wikipedia and Spark Notes is prohibited.

The book:

- Must have 250 pages
- Must have never been read by the student
- May be fiction or nonfiction
- Cannot be a movie

Use MLA or APA format
The report should include the following:

- Title /Author
- Publication information
- Genre
- Introduction
  - Overview of book without specific details
  - Broad information only
  - Thesis statement

Body

- What is the book about? Give specific details of the story; two or three paragraphs
- What do you think about the book? Give specific examples from the book.

Analysis and Evaluation

- Is the writing powerful, moving, difficult? Describe how the book impacted you.
- What are the strong and weak points of the book?
- Do you agree with the author's point of view? Why or why not?
- What is your impression from the book? Explain your reaction to reading the book.

Conclusion

- Overview of the writing—no new ideas
- Pull all the thoughts together and make a brief conclusion

Summary

Marginalization in education is nothing new. Racism is nothing new. The practices in education are not new, either. These factors have a powerful discord in education and on the students; particularly in an urban environment. Intentional practices of culturally relevant teaching can positively impact students and create lifelong learners. Additionally, the care and intention can reset the course for a student who was once thought lost. Imagine if someone had taken time with Alexander in the Introduction.

Teaching is a special art. It is the only profession that prepares all other professions. In that, teachers make decisions that impact the lives of children daily. Each day, it is the outlook of the teacher that gives the student another chance. As teachers, it is imperative that grudges are not held, that every day students are given the benefit of the doubt. A clean slate—and teachers give their all without prejudice. Can you do that?

CHAPTER FOUR

THE ROLE OF THE STUDENT

Parents

Parents are a critical part of the education process. Students are too. In the early years, parents are the most important factor for children to be successful in the learning environment. As a former teacher, I saw so many things that parents overlooked. As a parent, teachers are held to a higher standard—and expectation. Few parents think about their role in the education process. Parents are to prepare their children for success in school.

In elementary school, students need to come with the ability to:

- Recognize their first and last names
- Sit for several hours
- Stay in their space
- Recognize the alphabet and numbers
- Love to learn

This can be accomplished by creating a learning environment at home. Read to your children. Make everything about learning. In the grocery store, talk to your children about what is being bought. Recognize the colors, shapes, and whether it is a vegetable, fruit, healthful. Doing this, critical-thinking skills are developed. Children, when faced with questions, are thinking and forming sentences. Children who talk and speak well often become better readers. By questioning and discussing the fruit or other things found in the grocery store, parents can create a culturally balanced child. Where are the bananas grown? Where do we get kiwi? Discuss if these items come from their state, found in the United States, or were shipped from another country. While they may not be able to comprehend the miles or the location, it adds to their ability to understand that the world is greater than they are.

When parents drop off children to the day care center, they believe a teacher will teach their child—and they are right. However, parents are the first teachers. Parents, do you or are you willing to:

- Read daily to your child? In reading, are you focusing on the words and the background so the child can see the whole picture? Are you asking questions about the character, setting, and how the story is progressing?
- Play educational games with your child?
- Talk to your child?
- Teach your child how to sit at a desk? Hold a pencil, and sit for long periods without talking?

These are simple, but several students have not been socialized to learn in any environment.

Often as parents see their children through the elementary process, many are excited because the child is growing and becoming more independent. As children enter middle school, they need their parents more than ever. The change of two main teachers or one main teacher to a different teacher for every subject is almost traumatizing. Students entering middle school need:

- Accountability—how are you going to hold your child accountable?
- Structure
- Parent/Teacher relationship
- Schedule—children need structure; their weekdays need to have planned activities
- Minimized television time

Parents begin to distance themselves in middle school and become absent in high school. Students in high school need parents to become advocates for what is best for them. In elementary and middle school, parents are the guides and disciplinarians, and they pilot the process. High school shifts because the student is becoming their own person. In these years, parents need to know about end-of-grade tests, possible college entrance exams. Parents, are you willing to:

- Attend back-to-school night?
- Volunteer?

- Provide structure?
- Determine how you are going to hold your child accountable?
- Prepare for life after high school?

If parents and teachers work together in an honest effort to promote student success, the lives of students could possibly be transformed.

Students

The concepts of teaching and learning are not foreign to any educator. How and why, however, are vastly different. Each educator presents information differently. In reality, teaching and learning—how they are defined—how they are practiced, who the stakeholders are, and the influence of identified stakeholders are in constant discussion and research. Students are the constant focal point of how instructors become better and more impactful. In essence, it is a dual accountability and responsibility. Teachers come to teach—they have often planned and created more than one approach to learn a concept. Students, ask yourselves how you come to class. Are you unapproachable? Are you mean and intimidating? Are you a procrastinator?

As a former teacher, I have encountered so many excuses. Students with great potential flounder; fear of failure or laziness plague them. While some teachers can be off-putting or might not seek to establish a relationship, it is imperative that you, the student, come to class open and seeking to learn. As a student, are you willing to:

- Come with the understanding of respect?
- Read, study, and prepare for the class and the teacher?
- Put away technology if asked?
- Lose the attitude?
- Forgive the past? If you have been neglected or violated in learning environments in the past, this teacher did not participate in it. Practice forgiveness so your past does not hinder your future.

As you enter the classroom, make an attempt to create a relationship with your teacher. Check for cultural competency—and check your own biases.

STRATEGIES FOR READING AND WRITING

Bias Audit

Make a check under the column to show how you feel about each of the following:

Group	Positive	Negative	Undecided
Arabs			
Atheists			
Athletes			
Born-Again Christians			
Buddhists			
Californians			
Catholics			
Communists			
Conservatives			
Democrats			
Doctors			
Egyptians			
Elderly			
Honor Society			
Iraqis			
Jews			
Lawyers			
Liberals			
Muslims			
Nerds			
New Yorkers			
Protestants			
Republicans			
Secretaries			
Socialists			
Sororities			
Southerners			
Wealthy			
Welfare			
Working Class			

Look at your answers. Why do you think you feel the way you do? Where have your beliefs about these groups come from? What role do you think the media has had in your forming your opinions? Why?

Conflict

Conflict is traditionally the problem of the story. There is internal and external conflict. *Internal conflict* is a fight within someone—they are battling forces within their minds/beliefs. *External conflict* is a fight with someone or something from outside of one's self.

Types of Conflict

- *Man vs. Man*: A person is struggling with another person.
- *Man vs. Nature*: A person is struggling with natural elements— sharks, weather, any source of nature.
- *Man vs. Society*: A person is struggling against the cultural aspects of society; the ideals of society or trying to change the current societal method.
- *Man vs. Machine*: Not sure if this is "real" but perhaps the newest of the conflicts as several books and movies demonstrate a problem/ conflict/struggle with machines or things that aren't human, natural, or societal.
- *Man vs. Himself*: A person struggling with him- or herself to do what is necessary.

Conflict has five aspects, with several questions to each aspect.

1. PROBLEM
    a. What are the issues to be addressed?
    b. What are the conflicts to be resolved?
    c. Is there a policy or procedure contributing to this program?
    d. What systemic organizational issues does the problem illustrate?
    e. What features of the organization are fueling or sustaining conflicts?

2. PEOPLE
    a. Who are the key parties?
    b. What are the perspectives of the disputants?
    c. Do the parties represent the concerns of others who are like them?
    d. Who has a stake in keeping things as they are?

3. POWER
   a. How is power distributed?
   b. What power do individual disputants have?
   c. What do they have to gain or lose?
   d. Who most needs the conflict to be resolved?
   e. How will addressing/resolving this conflict affect the power structure of the organization?
   f. What are the politics of the situation?

4. POSITION/INTERESTS
   a. What is the dispute about?
   b. What interests and concerns does each group have?
   c. What organizational interests are reflected?
   d. What problems are reflected?

5. PROCESS
   a. What intervention possibilities exist?
   b. Which interventions are best suited to the concerns of the disputants?
   c. Is this cause for a systemic intervention?
   d. Which intervention will best lay the groundwork for a systemic intervention?
   e. What sort of systemic intervention will be most appropriate?

Four Major Types of Conflict

By observing the manner in which a character resolves or doesn't resolve a conflict, one can gain insight into the character's qualities, values, and personality.

1. Character's struggle against nature. When a character must overcome some natural obstacle or condition, a conflict with nature occurs.
2. Character's struggle against an antagonist. A struggle between two people is a common element in many works of literature. However, a conflict between two people is not always openly hostile.
3. Character's struggle against society. A struggle against society occurs when a character is at odds with a particular social force or condition produced by society, such as poverty, political revolution, a social convention, or set of values.
4. Struggle between competing elements within the character (internal conflict). Within a character, aspects of his or her personality may struggle for dominance. These aspects may be emotional, intellectual, or moral. For example, an emotional conflict would occur if the protagonist chose an unworthy lover over someone who is devoted. An

intellectual conflict could entail accepting or rejecting one's religion. A moral conflict might pose a choice between honoring family or country. Such conflicts typically leave the character indecisive and agitated. Even when such conflicts are resolved, the resolution may be successful or unsuccessful.

Remember: Conflict is a struggle between two opposing forces. To understand conflict in literature, become familiar with the key character terms "protagonist" and "antagonist."

Protagonist:
Antagonist:

Reading for Conflict

As you read a story:

1. Identify the main characters.
2. Decide what conflict they face.
3. Look for steps they take to settle that conflict.
4. See if the steps cause other conflict.
5. Watch for clues and try to predict what the characters will do.
6. Enjoy the buildup of suspense.
7. Put yourself in the story.
8. Decide if you would have solved the conflict the same way.

Context Clues

What do you do when you come across a word that is unfamiliar? Context clues offer the reader a way to understand the meaning of a word from the context:

- Not an exact definition
- Gives enough information for an approximate definition

There are several types of context clues:

Restatement

- Many authors redefine or restate key words to be sure readers understand.
- Definitions are introduced by the word or phrase "that is"; dashes, parentheses, and commas are other common devices to signal to the readers that restatement is being used.

Examples

1. In business, a great deal of information is passed through the grapevine, that is, an informal communication network.
   What does "grapevine" mean?
2. Stress, or feelings of worry, strain, and anxiety, can lead to physical problems.
   What does "stress" mean?
3. The velocity of growth—the rate or speed by which children change size over a period of time—varies greatly from child to child.
   What does "velocity" mean?

Contrast: Antonyms

- The context clue is often the telling of the opposite meaning of the word.
- This allows readers to see a different meaning of the word to understand its meaning.

Examples

1. To the public, she presented herself as an altruist. Her employees, however, knew her for what she was, a woman who cared only for herself.
   What does "altruist" mean?
2. In contrast to Professor Martinez, who was too strict, Professor Morrison was too lenient. Unfortunately, that creates another set of problems.
   What does "lenient" mean?

Example

- The author provides several examples of what the word means—there are no synonyms or antonyms

Examples

1. I'm always surprised by how *eccentric* she is. When people visit her, she talks to them from behind a curtain. When she meets them on the street, she hugs them as if they were old friends. Yesterday I saw her walking a leash without a dog.
2. For him, *deception* was a way of life. For instance, he lied about never being married before. He also lied about being an architect. He just couldn't resist trying to make people believe his stories.

General Knowledge

-   The reader's ability to use context depends on the situation or experiences

Example

1. As a lawyer, he owed his clients a good defense. But she was guilty, and the crime was so heinous, he was tempted to lose the case on purpose. *What does "heinous" mean?*

To review, the four common types of context clues are **Restatement** (provides definitions), **Contrast** (tells readers what the word doesn't mean), **Examples** (provides illustrations of the words), and **General Knowledge** (describes a familiar situation or experience).

There are other types of context clues, but these are the most used. Readers do not need to memorize the types, but do need to recognize when they are being used.

Main Idea

Objective: At the end of this session, students will have an understanding of how to locate the main idea by completing exercises of general and specific information.

The most helpful reading skill is the ability to find the author's main idea. It is the general idea that the passage or idea is about. The main idea is the author's general point; under it fits all the other material, which is made up of:

-   Supporting details
-   Examples
-   Reasons or facts

Main Idea

Poor grades in school can have various causes. For one thing, students may have money problems. If they need to work long hours to make money, they will have little study time. Another reason that might cause poor grades is relationship problems. A student may be unhappy over family problems or a lack of friends. That unhappiness can also harm schoolwork. A final cause of poor grades may be study problems. Some students have never learned how to take good notes in class or to manage their time. Without such skills, their grades are likely to suffer.

Locating the Main Idea

- Poor grades in school can have various causes (A)
- Students may have money problems (B)
- Students may not know how to study (C)
- Some students have never learned how to manage their time efficiently, or how to study a textbook (D)

The general statement that expresses the main idea of the passage is A! Poor grades in school can have various causes.

How did we find that answer?

Sentence A: The phrase "various causes" is a general one. It is broad enough to include all specific ideas mentioned in other sentences.

Sentence B: This sentence is only about one problem—money. It isn't enough to include all the problems listed. It is too specific. This sentence is a good supporting detail.

Sentence C: This sentence mentions only one specific cause—study problems, which does not include the other problems mentioned. This is another example of good supporting detail.

Sentence D: This sentence lists several study problems. It doesn't cover the other problems listed in sentences B and C. This sentence is a great one that makes the paragraph strong and provides another supporting detail.

General vs. Specific

General ideas are overlying ideas, very broad and vague. Specific ideas are supporting details that give information to build the general idea.

General term: Computers
Specific term: Dell, Mac, Apple

General term: Animal
Specific term: Rabbit, Cat, Dog
General term: Vegetable
Specific term: Carrot, Radish, Lettuce

General term: Emotion
Specific term: Sad, Happy, Discombobulated

How to Find the Main Idea

1. Establish a topic
    Who or what is this about?
    How do I relate this information?
    What is the central point?

2. Focus on the message
    What is the main idea that the author is trying to convey about the topic?
    What does the author want me to know about the topic?

3. Identify key supporting terms
    What are the important details?
    Answer the following questions:

    -   According to the passage ...
    -   The evidence given by the author is ...
    -   What are the major supporting details?
    -   What are the minor supporting details?

Questioning, one of our reading strategies, is very important in locating the main idea of any passage.

Narrative

Narrative writing:

- Is a storytelling process
- Is told from a particular point of view
- Makes a point
- Is filled with details, anecdotes
- Uses conflict and sequence
- Can be more casual and fun, shows style and creativity
- Features an introduction, states what kind of essay it is (but don't say, "This is a narrative essay about …")
- Can be about an event, recurring activity, personal experience, or an observation

Tells a Story

Reflection—remembering an event
Exploration—adventure
Events
People
Making observations of the present

Point of View

This is how the story is told
Can be in the first person (the use of "I" is acceptable)

Making It Good

Remember throughout the story:

- That nothing happens randomly
- To use images, metaphors
- To maintain style, tone, and point of view

In the opening:

- Show characters
- Show what's at stake

- Establish the setting
- Establish the conflict
- Set the tone of the story (happy, sad, etc.)

In the body of the work:

- Show the purpose of the obstacle/conflict/resolution
- Don't tell readers, show readers
  Example: (Don't) "He was loud and rude."
  (Do): "'Get outta my way, you jerk!' he screamed."

In the conclusion:

- Present a final conflict

Narrative Rubric

Your essay must:

- Establish and develop appropriate plot, setting, and point of view
- Include sensory details and concrete language to develop plot and character
- Use a range of narrative strategies
- Use correct grammar, punctuation, and sentence structure
- Have sentences that are completely formed
- Make sense

Poetry

What is poetry? Poetry is a form of written or oral language that is used to tell stories, express feelings, and give readers information. Poems can also be funny and fun to read.

Key Elements of Poetry

Form—the way a poem looks on the page
  Sound—poems depend on sound to help express meaning and motion
  Imagery—the use of words and phrases to create mental pictures; these words and phrases often appeal to the five senses

Figurative Language—language that is made up of words and phrases that present ordinary things in new ways

Reading Poetry

People often write poetry to express feelings. A poem's form, sound, imagery, figurative language, and speaker all work together to help the reader imagine the experience the poet is sharing.

Preview the poem and read it aloud a few times. Notice the form, shape, and if the poem has stanzas. Listen for rhymes and rhyme patterns.

Visualize the images. Create a mental picture of the images you find in the poem. Do they remind you of your own feelings? How do the images connect to the overall meaning of the poem?

Think about words and phrases. Think about how the poet's choice of words adds to the meaning or feeling of the poem. What is surprising? What evoked emotion in you?

Make inferences. Use your own knowledge and details (context clues) to make logical guesses and predictions about the meaning of the poem. Think about the speaker's attitude and personality.

Consider the theme. Ask: What message is the poet trying to send or help me understand?

APPENDIX

SELECTED READINGS

BY CHEVELLA WILSON

The Crux of the Matter

I'm angry.

Mad.

Like fighting mad ...

But what's new?

So many of my boys, black boys, have been killed. Some at the hands of another black man; others at the hands of white men ... police officers ... too many to name. It hurts.

But there's a curious case of this on—Ferguson feels different, hard, ugly, and vile. I know so many have written about it.

It hurts.

I am not sure what I can say that people have not already said ... so I won't.

We have a leadership issue in black America. Jesse went to Ferguson. Al went to Ferguson. Jamal went to Ferguson. I get it. At first, I did not like it ... but I get it. They are the people who are willing to be on the forefront of everything—they sacrifice their lives and their privacy to lead their community. We, the community, may not agree or like them. But they show up. Again, we might not like it, but they appear to care (for the camera)—but I believe in certain situations, Al and Jesse both care. Often it is not about the image, but the long sense of being there to help.

But I turned on the TV Tuesday night. I saw something that pissed me all the way off. Iyanla was on OWN in the streets of Ferguson mentoring men. Huh?

I love Oprah. I want to be interviewed by her—I want to be on the couch ... I have fallen in and out of love with Iyanla ... over the course of years, it is more love than hate. I see her purpose. I understand. I would love to be mentored by her and see her work.

I had a friend over, and he was stunned too. We watched in silence. Then he uttered, "There are some things men need to discuss with men. And women leading men is …" I sat in silence.

I feel the same way.

Yes, I am a feminist. Yes, I root for women and feel that we are equal and powerful and great. Often I know there are places I do not belong. As a woman, my feminine energy cannot prevail over the masculine energy. We work together. In the best of worlds, the feminine and masculine work together. He is strong, leader, protector. She is strength, powerful, yet knowing her "place." No, not kitchen and the bedroom, but understanding that a man can tell a boy-child the perspective of specific things because of his discovery. As women, we often forget we are dealt with differently in corporate, social, and every setting. Especially black women. We forget our men are more marginalized than we are.

I have seen Oprah and Iyanla discuss things with men and work with men on their "stuff" … I know of programs held by pastors and leaders that mentor and directly connect with men on all levels—social, economic, leadership, being fathers, Afrocentric, culture, drug problems … they have it covered. So why are Oprah and Iyanla so determined to touch men? They are powerful women. They have changed the face of how women are perceived. They are wonderful in what they do—fix women; empowering women … but men?

Where is Jesse? Al? Jamal? If they are true leaders, why aren't they trying to improve the lives of men? Why aren't they creating a mentoring circle? Or why aren't they improving the lives of men in their communities? Baltimore is dying—literally—voting practices are low, black-on-black crime is high, so many women are single mothers and leading their homes, schools are failing children—why not create a niche that provides the means to aid in these social ills? Jesse, Chicago is dying. More black men have died in Chicago than in Afghanistan … yet the mayor told the press not to ask him any more questions about that. Schools in low socioeconomic neighborhoods have closed—there are few, if any black-owned businesses in that part of town, the hopelessness and haplessness prevail so greatly that few see a future beyond their today. Why aren't Jesse, Al, and Jamal pooling their resources to aid in these communities?

I'm not hatin'.

I'm not singling these men out, necessarily.

I want men in every community to be more prevalent. Where are they? Why isn't our community creating leaders and training boys to be men? Why aren't our men teaching our boys—without regard of being family—how to be? If men began to show up at lunchrooms just to talk to boys, or show up in classrooms just to read, or become Big Brothers, or volunteer at golf/football/

basketball programs—and extend that to every facet of their lives. Yes, it takes time. Yes, it stretches the man beyond his potential and no, there is no immediate cash payout. But in the end, the boy-child is better, in the end, our communities are better. In the end our boys become men who give back, who are better readers and leaders, who can think and grow and do more ... they become protectors and not predators.

If it takes a village, where is ours?

Naturally Yours

I'm over the entire natural hair fight. I simply don't get it. I don't. I recall the exact day and time I decided to go natural. I walked into the salon to see my regular stylist and she suggested I needed a perm—it cost $90 and then told me the style would be $30. I got the perm, thinking I didn't need one, paid and left. I never, ever went back to her. Shortly thereafter, I met a wonderful stylist who could press hair—only—and it was wonderful.

I loved my hair. It was long, flowed, and I swear my bob style was the best thang going! People used to stop me on the street and ask about my hair. One night, on a date, a man told me, "I'd like to see your hair in its natural state." I explained proudly, "I am natural." It was like an alarm went off—everyone decided to chime in. I was not natural—pressed hair isn't natural hair. I was "cheating" and not "true to the natural community" ... further because I had color, I was told "natural means without dyes, colors and perms." Because of this, I didn't love myself; much less my culture. I was confused.

Every other culture wears their hair in its natural state. I don't want to hear about the Hispanics/Latinas getting their hair straightened. I don't want to hear anything about Jews or white women who are flat-ironing their hair. It is TOTALLY different. Completely. In their natural state, they still have the "look" of the so-called majority. In our process, sometimes we look different. Our styles and our hair is soft and fluffy to difficult and ... If it rains, LAWD—the texture of our hair can change very drastically. I have seen my own hair go from loose curls and bouncing and behaving to drawn up and I'm looking like Angela Davis. While nothing is wrong with that, let's face it, it scares people. That fear drives them to ask questions I don't want to answer.

In all of that, I also recall being very afraid to wear my hair naturally. I'd been addicted to creamy crack for so long—And I wanted to know if I'd still be "beautiful me" ... and if or how my friends, family, and co-workers would accept me. I finally did it—it was freeing and I loved it. I avoided rain like the plague and just learned to look at me differently. Most didn't say anything (you know what that means). Others, like my mother, wondered if I was gay, my father told me I was going to hell, and my friends just looked. Men told me I was beautiful, while others wouldn't date me because they didn't like my hair. One even told me I would be pretty with straight hair. I'll never forget attending GHOE (Greatest Homecoming on Earth) and an old friend, a man, an Omega, walked up to me and said, "You're beautiful. Simply beautiful. That style, those locs embrace your face and wow." I floated for the rest of the weekend, into the week. I want all of my sisters in the natural "fight" to feel that way, too.

Hair is an accessory. We make too much of it. If it all fell out—would our hearts change? Would we vote differently? Would we change our inner selves? No. It's just hair. Long, short, straight, or wavy—it is just hair. If yours is beautiful, I will compliment it and love it, too. It's just hair. Honestly, an older woman told me, "Girl, I have had plenty men ask me for p_$$%, but none have ever asked me for hair."

My Soul Needs Rest

I am deeply disturbed as I write this. I don't want any pictures. I don't want any video clips of his death—no news clips either. I don't want any words to a song. I want to use my words to really make readers feel and think this through. Again, a black male has been murdered. A life, which may be not as innocent as we would feel comfortable with, but a life—a man with a family. A man with a record. Still, a man. As I have reviewed several clips of his offensive death, sadly, The Boy watched, too. From an eight-year-old's perspective, he wanted to know what Eric Gardner had done so wrong to be choked to death. In that vein, I asked my FB friends, "What should Eric Garner have done?" The comments left me very upset. Angry-er. Yes, written like that.

Master did a number on us. It seems every single time our lifestyle, our community, our "us" (yes, written like that) the relationship the black community has with itself and its image is disheartening. Per the answers to my Facebook post, Mr. Gardner had been arrested several times ... he was doing wrong—he should have listened and not fought. But I didn't see a fight. I saw a man who was upset because he was being targeted (again).

This summer has been wrought with racial foolishness. The nice old man who owns the Clippers told his girlfriend how he felt about "us" ... Stephen A came to the rescue to tell us what we are doing wrong. For a moment, Stephen forgot he, too, is black—and he now, because of position, is a black man of privilege. White folk don't see him the same way they saw Trayvon, the young men at the gas station playing their music too loudly, or Mr. Gardner. Once in the tower of privilege, it's very easy to forget and harangue the public on how "black folk should act and acquiesce to make white folk feel comfortable."

I can't.

I can't.

I can't.

Honestly, initially, I did think Stephen A was right on point—and argued some folk down about it. But when my friend, an attorney, explained to me the black (his) male perspective, I understood. He explained that instead of admonishing the black community and giving lessons on how to make white folk more comfortable, Stephen A should have explained that everyone wears a hoodie—all people. Educated folk, tattooed folk, people who rob and steal—but what people have on should not make us judge them. Another friend explained, "We are hated from birth—people hate black men. They are taught we are evil, will rape, and kill, etc.—all because of our skin." While these two concepts may seem foreign to this piece, it isn't.

The relationship we have with our community is equated to that of the battered spouse syndrome. After being mistreated/beaten he or she returns to the abuser asking, "What can I do to stop being hurt?" All of us know the story—nothing. It is nothing we can do to really stop the abuse—but leave. The abused takes on the negative imagery the abuser has given. It is a train wreck to watch. As I idly watch the Black Community—we are that. Every time one of our children is harmed by a white man, we turn inward. Some blame Trayvon for being out after dark. Some blame him for wearing a hoodie. Some think the children (these were children) should have turned down the music—listened to their "elder"—and they all would be alive. When I showed my class the movie about Oscar Grant, several of them suggested had he not fought back, sat quietly, he would be alive. I was speechless. I was hurt.

At what point do we—the community—stand for our men? At what point is it not okay for a white man or any other to kill our children? Killing the men, the collective, they are killing dreams, killing hope—and making it very clear our lives are not equal to theirs. Every shooting or harsh treatment of our men brings out the argument, "Black-on-black crime in Chicago, Baltimore, Detroit, and other urban areas is high, but we get mad when a white man kills us." True … but I get offended every time I hear of a death of a black man. In that death, we have lost a leader, a father, the potential for greatness. Some think it is designed racism to ensure we end ourselves by ourselves—maybe. If that is true, at what point do we rally around our brothers and let them know of other options? At what point do we mentor, demonstrate, love, and guide them to and through the wilderness experiences?

Mentioning that concept, I am met with, "They have access to education …" and "I got out, why can't they?" Getting out now versus twenty years ago is very different. Several years ago, the traps were not as pronounced. The schools were still caring places, holding people (teachers, principals, guidance counselors) who gave a damn—even if your mother didn't. They had empathy and connections. In that era, people would send a "troubled" child to college and he or she would often find and manifest their potential. Now, all of these people come with preconceived notions about the paper trail they have read about said child. All too often our black males are caught in the poor school system with teachers who don't know enough about them to care or don't care enough to know. The cycle pushes them out of education and into the streets. There, they find a hustle. It isn't legal, it isn't right, but it allows them to feel like a man. They have money, they have means, they can provide.

When do we become alarmed that too many of our own are selecting the wrong path? Or are mistreated by the police? Or are not getting proper treatment from teachers, principals? The systems that once protected us now spew our youth out before actualizing their true potential. When does the community rally around the notion of us—if I made it, will he and she make it, too?

It is my hope our community will return to itself—a center of love and support for all. In seeing the death of Mr. Gardner, my son, The Boy is forever spooked. Just when he thought it was okay to be—he's just getting over Trayvon and the others in Florida—he realizes it may never be okay to be. Just when he is comfortable at being a child, he has not-so-gentle reminders that someone is always lurking. At any point, he could be wrongly identified. Then killed.

Beat Me? Please

It seems most of the country or Facebook, at least, has been consumed with the death of Bianca Tanner. Bianca Tanner was an elementary school teacher in Greensboro, NC. She went missing in early June. Initially, her boyfriend was not a person of interest—until the authorities realized he and his friends were lying. Then they stopped cooperating … . Then the boyfriend (she recently moved to Charlotte to be with him) went missing. We (especially the BGLO community) were upset he was caught and photographed in a Kappa shirt (but that's another story). When I learned of this, I immediately wondered who and how her sister circle helped or ignored her.

First, I was excited "we" were being featured in a missing-person story. Then it hit me, she probably won't come home—alive. As the story unfolded, I knew. A nasty feeling in the pit of my stomach forcing it to churn, I knew. Once I heard of his past transgressions, of the women he beat and abused previously—I knew. Maybe I knew because she is a friend, an aunt, someone I knew in a past life. We have all watched *The Burning Bed* and seen Gina get beat up on "A Different World" and various other shows that easily dissolve the problem in twenty minutes. Yes, I'd venture to say we all know someone who has been a victim of domestic violence. In each situation, what do we do? Are we the type to turn our head, pass judgment, or help?

Help comes with a cost. Often the victim will lash out at you—out of embarrassment, hurt, and pain. Usually they are not able to emotionally leave, let alone physically leave. I have two dear friends and an aunt I supported through their ordeals. In each case, there was a friend or family member who was callous, hurtful, and judgmental. Instead of being helpful, they asked, "How can a woman let a man treat them like that?" And continued with comments like, "She must like it if she stays." When I watched my friends endure, one would call me at all times of the day/night/ afternoon after her then-boyfriend abused her. She had so many friends, I wondered why she always called me. Once she explained, "I have called others. They told me they wouldn't get involved." I was confused, hurt. With that friend, I openly talked about plans of leaving, getting help, and even stood with her when she was ready.

The system is not kind to women or people who have been battered. When we sought to get a gun license, we learned it would take more than 30 days. When asked about a restraining order, it would take a court date AND 45 days to implement. The officer noted, "It's a backlog in the courts, so your date won't come until spring." It was January.

Abuse is more about the insecurity of the abuser. Usually they are insecure and seeking power and control. Because the person they are with is strong, willful, beautiful—they feel they need to break that spirit and dominate. It is a sickness. Rarely do anger management programs help. In helping, it is best to know the victim needs to leave.

All of this to ask when someone is hurt and is finally brave enough to ask for your help, what are you going to do? Are you going to gossip about him/ her or really listen and then provide avenues to help? I deeply wish I knew Bianca. In spite of her being an educator and graduating from my beloved NCAT, our paths did not cross. She seems to have been a beautiful spirit gone too soon. Domestic violence is real—it hurts. Please help. Please.

CPSIA information can be obtained
at www.ICGtesting.com
Printed in the USA
LVOW02s2117201215
466902LV00004B/9/P

9 781634 871327